The Declassified Adoptee Essays of an Adoption Activist

By Amanda H.L. Transue-Woolston

Published by,
CQT Media And Publishing, and
LGA Inc.

Written by Amanda H.L. Transue-Woolston

Edited by Julie Stromberg

Foreword by JaeRan Kim

ISBN 13: 978-0-9885858-2-9

Dedication & Acknowledgements

It is with heartfelt gratitude that I extend my deepest appreciation to the people in my life who have supported me along the way.

Thank you to my families by birth, adoption, and marriage for helping shape who I am today.

Thank you to my social work professors at West Chester University and at Bryn Mawr College for creating a nurturing environment for me to unfold as an activist and grow personally and professionally.

Thank you to my dear friends, fellow activists, and allies in the adoption community for supporting me along the way.

This book is dedicated to my children. May you always know who you are, where you come from, and where you are headed in life.

Table of Contents

Foreword by JaeRan Kim

When I first began my blog, Harlow's Monkey, in 2006 I was part of a small community of adoptee bloggers writing about adoption from a point of view that was largely missing – that of the adopted person. For some time I mostly read blogs by other transracial adoptees. Then one day I stumbled upon The Declassified Adoptee, after learning about Amanda's post "Dear Fellow Christian, It's Not the Same Adoption," a topic I also have been interested in, and written about, for a long time. In reading Amanda's post I knew I had stumbled up on a kindred spirit. Amanda is not a transracial or intercountry adoptee, but we speak the same language about the experience of being adoptees and we share the same passion for prioritizing the voices of those that are often suppressed or missing in the conversation. In addition we have many other commonalities – we are both moms to two wonderful kids, we are both social workers, and we are similarly called to advocacy work. And we both have supportive partners who stood by us when came up out of the "adoption fog," began to search for our birth families and fought for our civil right to our original birth certificates and adoption information. I was thrilled to meet Amanda in person when we, along with a powerhouse of other adoptees from around the country, met in Washington DC in 2012 to advocate for adoptees with the Congressional Coalition on Adoption Institute (CCAI). Amanda was an impressive speaker and made a lasting impression on everyone in the room.

The adoption "triad" is not an equilateral triangle. As in real life, the narratives and voices represented in blogs, media outlets and in traditional print are dominated by adoptive parents. If one were to draw the geometric shape of the adoption triad in terms of how society solicits, listens to and values experiences it would look more like a scalene triangle with no equal sides – the longest side being the adoptive parents, the shortest side the first family, and the adoptee somewhere in the middle. Adoptees are, by our very experience, always seemingly in the middle.

As Arundhati Roy put so succinctly, "there's no such thing as the 'voiceless.' There are only the deliberately silenced, or the preferably unheard." Adoptees and first parents have been publicly speaking out about their experiences since the days of the orphan trains and the Indian Adoption Project. Yet for too long, both in the adoption world and in greater society, adult adoptee and first parent voices have been silenced and unheard. Adoption professionals, those who have the greatest need for our expertise, have often been the most silencing. In my early professional career an adoption professional once said to me, "Just because you were adopted, it doesn't make you an expert in adoption." I disagree – adoption would not exist without the adoptee. We are the experts in our own experience. And let's not forget that the greatest reforms in adoption practice and policy have come from those who lived adoption – adoptees, first families and adoptive parents.

This book is an intervention to correct the over-dominance on adoptive parent narratives about adoption and what adoption means to a person. Amanda has a way of presenting her position in a way that is persuasive and often challenging to the status quo and yet absent of the personal attacks and deflection that is often present on social media these days. Although adoption is the creation of a legal relationship between a parent and a child, those of us who live this life know better – adoption is not an event, it is a lifelong journey; it is not about the creation of a legal relationship, but rather the creation of a personal relationship. These core truths are embodied in each essay of this book.

Through these essays, Amanda calls for a more equitable and humane conceptualization of adoption through her observations about adoption, experiences living adoption, and advocacy work. Her writing is clear, measured, and thought provoking. You will come away from these essays thinking more deeply about a topic than you did before you opened the pages. In addition, you will feel Amanda's deep value for the dignity and worth of all her fellow travelers who have been deeply touched by the adoption experience.

JaeRan Kim, MSW, PhD Candidate
Center for Advanced Studies in Child Welfare, University of Minnesota

Introduction

This book was born of my blog. With several hundred posts to date, I decided it was time to collect my favorites and edit them to be published together as a collection of essays. I feel blessed for the opportunity of this book project. It is a possibility of which I had never dreamed.

The Declassified Adoptee blog began as an effort to chronicle the experience of searching for my original family. After I reunited, I changed the focus of the blog to write about adoption and intersecting social justice issues. Readers picking up my writing for the first time may wonder, "How does this author feel about adoption?" and "What are her experiences within adoption?" I hope to answer these questions while putting this collection of essays into context.

For a very long time, the only thing my adoptive parents and I knew about my pre-adoption life, family, and identity came from a paragraph-long agency narrative. Although I am adoption's client as an adoptee, I was not permitted to see my own file held by my adoption agency. In 1999, the state of my birth passed a law allowing adult adoptees the ability to access their original birth certificate and adoption files with minimal restrictions. When I turned 24, I figured out how to navigate this harrowing process. In 2009, I became part of a very small percentage of U.S. born adopted persons to access both my original birth certificate and my adoption file. What was once top secret information, my original identity, was now "declassified."

If you spend just a bit of time immersed in adoption community culture, you will notice that we are often quick to categorize each other into one of two diametrically opposed sides: "pro-adoption" or "anti-adoption." This false dichotomy ignores the deeply personal and complex experiences of all those affected by adoption. It also fails to encompass the phenomena of ambivalence transforming to wisdom when a person gives meaning to their hardship and lives a beautiful life. When we discuss difficult topics, I think we should remember that adoption is an institution, it is not a person. We should be able to talk about adoption, and how it affects people in both good ways and bad ways, without feeling insulted as people.

I am pro-human. I support healthy and positive interaction between human beings and the institutions that impact their lives. I view adoption no differently than I view any other institution, like marriage, religion, heath care, or education, to name a few. Institutions include some people while excluding others. Some people excel within a given institution while others are left behind due to political and systemic barriers. Institutions contain stratified systems of benefits and privilege. An institution may provide benefits to some while harming others. Adoption is not free from the same general strengths and challenges that institutions are known to encompass.

My ultimate goal is to challenge the common belief that adoption is a mysterious process that exists within a vacuum, and, therefore, should abide by its own rules and have its policies go unquestioned. Adoption does not occur in a vacuum. Adoption is a social institution that impacts the lives of human beings, including the lives of those in incredibly vulnerable populations. As such, we have to critique it. We have to discuss the experiences of those who live adoption. We have to face what is not working. We will fail those who need help most if we do not investigate how adoption impacts their lives.

If you want to know what it is like to be adopted, you must ask those who are adopted. There is no replacement for the invaluable adoptee narrative within adoption. However, I encourage all people to gain an interest in adoption issues and become an ally to adoptees. You do not have to be an adoptee, an adoptive or original parent, an adoption professional or a family member of an adoptee to have an opinion on adoption and want to work for change. If you understand human rights and social justice frameworks and how to apply them to adoption, then you are more than equipped to assess the fairness of adoption concepts, policies, and practices and stand together with us as change-makers.

This book is not a memoir. Rather, I examine my own experiences while pulling back the lens and confronting the adoption concepts that I have encountered. It is true that adoptees are experts on their own stories. However, I believe we must also assert our place at the table in the discussion of adoption as an institution.

This book will not tell you how to adopt or give an exquisite layout of the adoption process or global adoption issues. My writing reflects my experiences as an adopted person from my type and era of adoption. Every piece contained in this book was a part of my transition from being silent about being adopted to speaking about it with confidence.

By publishing this book, I make the bold assumption that there are others who may relate to or be empowered by what I have written. I have purposely included the essays that readers have qualified as most meaningful to them based on feedback. Throughout the years, readers have informed me that they have read these pieces on the floors of adoption hearings, have mailed them to family members of adoptees to expand their understanding of adoption, and have sent them to adoption agencies to encourage greater access to post-adoption support.

I do not encompass the entire adoption experience nor do I attempt to speak for everyone. I have contextualized this book by including my biographical statement at its conclusion. I do not write exclusively for people who think just like I do or who share my worldview. My own personal views are evolving each day as I work to be consciously aware of my own beliefs and biases and find my own way in this world. I am not just an activist. I am a storyteller. I am a listener and cherisher of others' stories. I am a person navigating reunion despite tough conception circumstances. I am an adoptee parenting biological children and learning to explain adoption to them. If universality, catharsis, empowerment, or peace are what you find here, I will consider this book's purpose well-served.

"All of these lines across my face.
Tell you the story of who I am.
So many stories of where I've been.
And how I got to where I am.
But these stories don't mean anything.
If you've got no one to tell them to."

--Brandie Carslile

Part One: Adoption Observations

"Those who do not have power over the story that dominates their lives, the power to retell it, rethink it, deconstruct it, joke about it, and change it as times change, truly are powerless, because they cannot think new thoughts."--Salman Rushdie

Names of individuals mentioned in this book have been changed to respect their privacy.

How to Listen to an Adoptee
Without getting offended

After almost half a decade of discussing adoption policy and practice, I have had the opportunity to receive a lot of feedback. Although the response to my voice has been overwhelmingly positive, I have noticed a great need for a better reception of adult adoptee voices. Think about it. When children are adopted, they are relatively voiceless. We may not hear about adoption from an adoptee until 18 or more years after their adoption took place. It seems like society doesn't expect to hear from adoptees. When we start speaking out, it is not always well-received. Everyone needs to acknowledge that the voices of adoptees make adoption better. We can prepare ourselves to listen to what they have to say.

Reading, or hearing about, other people's perceptions about adoption is not always easy. Adoption is so deeply personal to those who live it. Even though another person's experience may be different, when adoption is involved, it still may evoke an emotional reaction within ourselves in response. Often times, the personal discomfort brought about by reading a discussion on adoption, or experiencing something difficult about being adopted, must be addressed first before the message can be heard. Here are some concepts I keep in mind when reading another person's story that readers of adoptee stories should keep in mind too.

Adoption is an institution. It is not a person. Adoption impacts the lives of children and vulnerable people everywhere. It also impacts the lives of adoptive parents and original parents. We need to discuss its strengths and challenges in order to make it better. We cannot do this if we take everything said about the institution as a personal insult.

Never talk someone out of sharing his/her grief or joy. There is a time and a place to talk about pain. If a personal blog or story about their experience of being adopted is not the time or place, when or where is?

Be aware. Is asking an adoptee to tone it down or telling adoptees that they are not the only people with problems, really about the adoptee? Or is it about making yourself more comfortable with what they have to say?

They are not you and you are not them. Their story is not your story or the story of your loved ones. Their loved ones are not your loved ones. When it is not your story, you cannot direct how it gets told. You can listen, understanding how their narrative is not yours, while still learning from them when their words or experiences do apply or help. It is also not just about what you can learn from them, but about how you can support them in return.

None of us get it right all of the time. Years ago, I was not ready to hear the narratives of other adoptees. I was not ready to really listen or treat their stories with care. Guilty as charged. I needed to investigate what being adopted meant to me so that I, in turn, could both learn and contribute as a part of the overall adoptee community. With gratitude for how others have treated my stories with kindness, I have sought to build empathy with those who live and experience adoption. Adoptees, original parents, adoptive parents, and extended families – we all have different roles and perceptions in adoption. But first and foremost, we are human beings. A little human kindness goes a long way.

Adoptees did not ask to be a bridge between two worlds and two communities.

But they are.

They did not ask to be living proof that non-biological relationships can be successful.

But they are.

It is not their job to teach others what being adopted is like.

But they will.

So now we must listen.

Being "That" Adoptee
The one that everyone "knows," but doesn't really understand

"Adopted adults should not be singled out and queried unless they have volunteered themselves as a bridge -- and even then there are boundaries that must be respected."-- Terra Trevor

Adoption always seems to find its way into everyday conversations, at least for me. One especially unexpected time was while I was getting my hair trimmed. I was nine months pregnant at the time and the very young female stylist expressed concern that I would "pop" while she was cutting my hair. "Well, if those are new shoes, you might want to step back a few feet," I replied. Her eyes grew wide and her mouth formed a surprised "O." She had not caught onto my sarcasm.

While snipping the ends of my long brown hair, she chattered on about the horrors of childbirth and how she knows she just will not ever have babies because they will be too big. She asked me how big I thought my baby was. I told her I was not quite sure. She wanted to know how big I was when I was born. This information would surely tell me how big my baby would be. I gave my usual reply at the time, "I don't know. I'm adopted." Then she said it, the phrase that every adoptee has heard at least once in their lifetime. "My friend's sister is adopted and she loves it."

The conversation ended there with an "oh, ok" from me and a change of subject. The "I know an adoptee who…" phrase teeters precariously on the line of ventriloquism. Do they really know how their friend or acquaintance feels about being adopted? Should they really be sharing this information on this person's behalf? And what does it have to do with me now that I have told you that I am adopted? There is very little I can say in response without the conversation going to a place that is uncomfortable. When you challenge someone's perception of what they think being adopted is like – or assume that it can be summed up into one phrase such as "loves it" – this usually ends with the person professing to know more about being adopted than an adoptee does.

Here is what our friends, loved ones, and acquaintances need to know.

Sometimes the "I know an adoptee..." phrase is used to dismiss whatever a given adoptee is saying about his or her own narrative, especially if it is negative. Searching adoptees may encounter this if they disclose to someone that they are searching. The person might say in return, "I know someone who is adopted and she's never wanted to search. Being adopted never bothered her!"

This sends a micro-aggressive message that adoptees who search are "bothered" by being adopted. It also sends the message that the conversation with this person is not a safe place to talk about the complexities of being adopted. We also know from research that search and reunion are absolutely no indication that an adoptee had a bad adoption experience or does not appreciate their adoptive parents. This micro-aggression is, plain and simple, a hurtful stereotype.

I have asked people how they know an adoptee in their life feels a certain way about being adopted. One of the most common replies is, "Well, she never talks about it."

This makes me chuckle. For I am an adoptee with plenty of thoughts on adoption, both positive and negative, that I do not always volunteer to share with the friends of my siblings or the stylist at the hair salon. To some people that I have encountered, I am "that adoptee." I am one who has no thoughts, feelings, or ambiguity when it comes to adoption, and they know this because "I never talk about it." As readers likely know by now, I actually have plenty to say.

My family members are not all privy to the intricacies of my feelings on adoption and being adopted. I have nothing to hide, but I am also aware that my thoughts impact others. Talking about being adopted requires an adoptee to delve into topics that remind their adoptive family that they are not biologically related to the adoptee. I never wanted my family to think that I was not proud of my membership in their family. I also did not wish to remind my parents of their struggle to have a biological child; I knew their infertility hurt them.

It is best to try to move on, is it not, and to not force people to dwell on the past? As my friend, and fellow adoptee, Pastor Deanna once said, "What seems like the past for others is the present and future for the adoptee." Being adopted is not something that I could write off as a single event in January of 1986 in the judge's chambers on a cold New Jersey day. The uniqueness of simultaneously being a daughter of two separate families is something relevant to me each and every single day.

Growing up, I hardly ever talked about being adopted with my friends. I did not have very many friends who were adopted, and I likely felt that my biologically-raised friends would not really understand how I felt. Since I was still trying to figure out how exactly it is that I felt about being adopted myself, I did not see adoption as a topic I needed to spend a great deal of time dwelling upon. The closed-nature of my adoption magnified this for me. It was simply overwhelming for me to ponder endlessly on a topic that I thought I would never have the opportunity to know more about.

Looking back, I wish I would have confided in friends more. The fact of the matter is, I did not. To them, I was the friend who "never said anything about being adopted."

Even my adoption agency does not have an accurate understanding about the intricacies of my adoption experience. I contacted them by email for the first time, over twenty years after my adoption, to seek search and reunion assistance. Believing my agency was my only lifeline when it came to finding out my original mother's identity, I was wary of saying something that would ruin my chances of accessing my agency files. By wanting to search, I feared they would see me as an adoptee who was unhappy with her adoptive family. I wrote to them giving them the best and most cheery impression of being adopted.

They were quite impressed with my report, and asked if they could share it with others. Afraid I would ruin my chances of accessing information, I gave them permission. My ambivalence-free write-up of the adoption experience is probably floating around on an agency pamphlet somewhere or being read from a list of others at agency presentations. But it was not how I really felt.

The beauty of the adoptee community and the collective experience of being adopted is that not every adoptee views being adopted in the same way as any other adoptee. Everyone is different and everyone's voice and experience matters. There is no one cookie cutter mold that defines what being adopted is or that can be used to exclude other adoptee narratives from "counting."

The loved ones of adoptees are part of the adoption experience. But at the same time, they still do not know what it is like to walk in our shoes. This is why opening our minds, ears, and hearts to adoptees is necessary in order to understand what the adoptee community is really saying and what they need. Instead of shutting down one adoptee based

18

on what have been told by another, expand the dialogue. By accepting the narratives of adoptees, even those narratives that may challenge our perceptions and make us uncomfortable, the average everyday adoption conversation can become a safe place for adoptees to share and inform.

Do you know someone who never says anything about being adopted? They may be thinking about it more than you realize.

Adoption is Not Salvation
Why Christians should stop repeating this metaphor

Every Christian has heard this phrase at least once, "We're all adopted!" Spending kindergarten through high school in a Christian school, at church and youth group, and my first year of college at a Christian institution, I have heard it my fair share of times. As someone who has experienced adoption very literally, I have had to ask myself what being adopted by God means to me. As a Christian, this is a concept that I have had to talk out and reason through because it never sat well with me. Are adoptees "saved" through adoption just as sinners are saved by God?

The very basic message of Christianity is that God's people are sinners saved by grace. Christians believe that we are redeemed from the ultimate separation from God by Jesus' death on the cross in order to unite with God in heaven. As believers, we are called the brothers and sisters of Christ, co-heirs with him and the sons and daughters of God.

When viewing adoption on the surface, adoption does appear to provide a fitting metaphor for salvation. English translations of the Bible even use the word "adoption" to describe Christ's redemptive act. Although, I will argue that the adoption the early Christians knew is much different than the adoption we experience today.

When Christians compare adoption to salvation, they need to take a deeper look as to how the two concepts conceivably compare to truly understand the message that they are sending. In the metaphor of adoption as salvation, the origins and original parents of the adoptee play the role of hell. The innocent child plays the role of the fallen sinner who needs salvation. The adoptive parents represent Jesus, or God, who redeem the unworthy sinner.

Perhaps this is an easier concept to repeat when the only names and faces most predominantly visible in adoption discourse are those of the adoptive parents. What Christians need to know is that our original families are real people who may have faced struggles in their lives that exceeded their power to overcome at the time of our adoption. They are not "hell." They are valuable jewels of God, made in his image, and the crown of his creation just like any other human being.

Likewise, the question must be asked: what had I done wrong as a newborn baby in order to be justifiably compared to a spiritually redeemed sinner? The idea of adoption should be that all children are entitled to identity, love, care, food, clothing, health care, education, protection, and freedom. Children are entitled to these rights as a matter of being human and because they are vulnerable beings. When adults come together on behalf of a child to meet their human rights, it is not "redemption" of an undeserving individual. It is justice, long overdue, to the innocent child. In light of this fact, it becomes irreverent to the rights of children to refer to adoption as their "redemption" or "salvation."

I prefer to compare salvation to adoption reunion because it is a spiritually more positive portrayal of those connected to adoption. After all, we are the prodigal son that returned home, the coin that was missing from the purse, and the sheep that became lost. We have always been a part of God's original family for we cannot become prodigal, missing, or lost unless we belonged in the first place. Our families, whomever we identify as family – whether it be the original family, the adoptive family, or God's family – are ours to call home. We have never stopped belonging to God or our original families; we were simply lost for a little while.

"Better Off" Not Knowing
Empowerment in spite of your narrative's tragedy

I once took my lunch break in a small diner on the outskirts of a rather depressed town. I munched on a sandwich while enjoying the harmony of clinking glasses, forks tapping against plates, and spoons chiming as they swirled through cups of coffee. The stream of light that poured in from the window made my hand feel warm as the sun cast its beams across my paperwork. One of many news shows attempting to forecast the presidential election was humming lowly on the flat screen that adorned the boldly painted stucco wall. The gentleman at the table across from me was engaging a woman who was sitting across the room from him in conversation. The television screen suddenly broadcasted something about the latest abortion debate and a loud conversation between the two ensued.

"I do not think women should be able to have abortions," the woman called from across the dining room. That's a life and you shouldn't just be able to get rid of it!"

"I agree!" the man bellowed back. "Except when a woman is raped. I mean, can you imagine how awful it is to be one of those rape babies?"

Apparently, the man felt the compelling need to qualify his originally stated opinion. The woman, now chewing with sandwich poised in front of her mouth, nodded her head in a fashion that suggested wholehearted agreement. I sighed and wished the two would realize that women's privacy and choice in health care extended far beyond how terrible either of them must think it is to be me – a person conceived from rape.

I cannot help to notice a theme in these discussions. It is the idea that it is horrible to be this kind of person and not that kind of person, and it suggests that there are different kinds of people whose humanity is not equal to other humans. In this instance, it is based on conception circumstances.

So the question is often posed in other discussions, "Should we tell an adoptee about their conception circumstances or about their origins if they are particularly painful?" After all, who wants to find out that you are in that category of person which made my two accidental lunch companions feel so disgusted?

As an activist for transparency and access to information in adoption, I have had people ask me if I would want to know if I had been conceived from rape. They assume adoptees should not access their pre-adoption information because what they find is bound to be terrible. I suppose they have forgotten that human problems and tragedy do not exist outside of adoption.

It is a little too late for me to avoid finding out my conception circumstances. Believe it or not, I am still a happy person with a beautiful life. So I respond with my classic phrase, "I am an adult. I will decide what I am better off not knowing."

This what we should value, right? Self-determination? We should acknowledge that everyone deserves the truth, especially about their own lives, and that it is not up to others to tell us what we can and cannot know about ourselves.

I completely understand how much "I will decide what I am better off not knowing" borders on rhetoric. For how can you decide if something was good or not good for you to know until after you have already been told? I will argue that this is not a judgment that is made completely on hindsight. After all, there are things that I chose not to know about my origins.

I know who my biological father is. (Or was, rather. He died when I was 18.) I know my heritage from his side of the family. I know his family medical history. I have a relationship with his sister. I know his age and my mother's age at the time of my conception. I learned the details of my conception, at the age of 14 when my adoptive mother felt that I was old enough to know. For me, age 14 was the right time to be told.

When I reunited, my original mother told me that she felt it was important for me to be able to ask questions and to know anything about my biological father, or what happened to her, if it would bring me any closure. My aunt expressed the same. I asked them nothing and I think it really surprised them. I already had closure. I personally felt fine with the amount of information that I had. I did not need to know more information, but it is important to understand that I was able to make this decision for myself.

Should people have wanted to hide my conception circumstances from me, I am not sure where the truth would have begun or the omissions would have ended. Or how answers to my questions based on what was omitted could have been answered with anything but a lie or yet another omission.

When I asked about my biological father, which I rarely did, my parents would say, "We'll discuss that when you're older." When I was older, had they continued to omit what they knew, I might have felt that there was something I had to be ashamed about that they did not want to tell me.

If I had not known that I was adopted, I never would have asked those questions. However, that would have required my parents to omit the truth or lie to me altogether. The family medical history that would have been given to my doctors would not have actually been mine. I would potentially have used it to make decisions about tests and my health care. I would have never had the opportunity to seek reunion and information about my biological roots. My children would likely have never known that their mother is adopted and would never have the opportunity to know both of their heritages. This is a legacy that would have been passed forward to generations.

Not telling me the truth would have not only limited my knowledge about myself, it would have limited my ability to make decisions for myself due to lack of information.

Yes, there are some details I chose not to know. Ultimately, it is not the quantity of information or the level of detail passed along that is important to me. What is important was that no one lied to me. No one second-guessed my personal strength and resiliency in being able to handle tough information. No one decided for me what I was "better off" not knowing. No one side-stepped my story, tiptoed around it on egg shells, lied, or omitted huge chunks of information sending the message that I have something to feel ashamed about. In light of none of us having post-adoption support, I am so proud of how my parents and original mother have handled my narrative.

The fact that withholding information from adoptees has become the legal norm in the United States sends a widespread message that adoptees, by being adopted, automatically have something to feel ashamed about. The fact that your first answer to the request for your own information from your government or your own client file at an agency is, "No, but here's some red tape and bureaucracy for you to navigate," sends the message that we have something about which to be ashamed. It places unequal value on our humanity. After all, who wants to find out they were a "rape baby?"

I do fight for transparency and truth in adoption because I believe it is the best way to ensure honest and ethical practices and uphold the civil, human, and children's rights for all involved. Ultimately, it is not about giving people information they do not want or forcing someone to know something they do not want to know. It is about empowering them to make the choice to receive the information if they feel it is important to them.

Feeling Blamed
Why it's hard for loved ones to listen when we talk about adoption

Exhausted and sweaty from delivering my baby, I laid in the hospital bed. I was flanked on each side by a gorgeous doctor and a stunning vision of Jennifer Love Hewitt who was apparently my nurse. I remember my mind doing some sort of "mom gymnastics" as I gazed at this little baby on my chest. I glanced over every part of him to make sure he was OK while bursting into a sudden realization of motherhood. I could not help but notice that when he opened his mouth to cry, something seemed odd with his tongue. I felt concerned yet simultaneously ashamed of myself for noticing that something seemed not-quite-right with this perfect child.

The nurses did not seem concerned about my son's tongue. They were busy making other arrangements to transfer me to the post-delivery part of the maternity floor. Later on I was told that he had a "tongue-tie," which means his frenulum is so short, it makes it difficult for him to lift his tongue. I was informed that a "tongue-tie" can interfere with breastfeeding and speech development, but not to worry.

I started worrying when I had trouble breastfeeding him while still in the hospital. Every shift change brought a new nurse to my room with yet another breastfeeding technique. I grew increasingly overwhelmed as I barely mastered one technique before I was instructed to try a new one.

One of the pediatricians told me that "tongue-tie" is genetic, and asked us if we have any relatives with a short frenulum. My husband quickly absolved his genes from causing our son's near-immobile tongue. He knows his genetic relatives, his aunts, uncles, cousins, and grandparents. No one in his family has a problem with their tongue. I wanted to scurry beneath the bed sheets and hide my reddening face. It had to have been me, the not-reunited-mystery-genes adoptee who had gone and had a baby despite not knowing half of the genetic predispositions.

No one had to say anything. I assumed the blame.

The suggestion of a genetic cause coupled with the fact that I did not know anything about my own genetics made me feel indirectly blamed. As a mother, I did what mothers do and blamed myself. Not because I had really done anything wrong, but because my son was facing a challenge and I was not quite sure how to make everything better for him.

More than a year later, a professor of mine touched on this topic in a social work class. She stressed the importance of anticipating how parents will assume blame for challenges that their children face. This preparatory empathy should guide us in talking with parents about their children, making sure to encourage and empower them. I immediately looked back on the day and saw myself lying in that hospital bed, engaging in my very first self-blaming experience of parenthood.

The concept of blame resonates with me in my own adoption experience. One of the deepest difficulties of sharing adoption loss and grief is the fact that our parents and families may feel very much blamed. They may feel they are to be blamed for not knowing how to take the grief away or how to have prevented it in the first place. My adoptive mother once expressed guilt over adopting me in response to my grief. "Amanda, should we not have adopted you then?" She wanted to know. In reality, I was a little baby waiting in foster care. Adopting me did nothing to facilitate my loss.

Likewise, original parents may blame themselves for adoptee grief and loss. When I reunited, I faced the task of sharing my adoption-related grief with a mother who never wanted to surrender me to adoption in the first place. When I share my feelings of loss with my original mother, I am conscious of how what I share may conjure those feelings of powerlessness that she felt when I was born.

As a reunited adoptee, I had to consciously decide between withholding my feelings in an attempt to manage the emotions of others and being honest. I chose to trust my loved ones to understand my heart. Blame may be what they feel, but I am not blaming them. Ultimately, trusting them was the right choice. Whatever blame they felt has not become a roadblock to further dialogue and openness in my relationships.

As a parent, I have learned that I must acknowledge the moments in time where I feel at fault for any challenge's my children face. However, I must never allow these emotions to hinder my children from coming to me for support and being honest with me about how they feel about any given life experience. As an adoptee, this is a continuous practice in my relationships. I must be honest about how I am feeling and sensitive to how my loved ones may feel as a result. This sensitivity on my part must be delicately balanced with acceptance from my families, never to be barred or talked out of sharing grief. The bottom line when communicating with adoptees? Your first assumption should not be that they are blaming you or anyone else for their feelings; assuming that adoption discourse is about "blame" just shuts people down.

Like One of Their Own
Being "their own" instead of "kind of like it"

One afternoon, I had the privilege of watching the
performance of a talented First Nations dance troop. During a
brief break between dance routines, one of the dancers was
asked by the event host if he would like to tell the audience
anything. I found my eyes scanning the room as the dancer's
did. It was a sea of mostly white faces. He replied, "I'm a
normal person. I'm a real person, just like you."

Tears welled in my eyes and a sense of injustice gnawed its
way into my chest. White people view themselves as
cultureless, colorless, and normal while allowing themselves
the unlimited freedom to self-invent. People of color are
viewed as being bound to stereotypical behaviors and cultural
practices that a racist society abnormalizes and a colorblind
culture lauds itself for overlooking. He was there sharing his
culture with us that day, and he was aware of how weird,
exotic, and outside of U.S. culture he may be perceived.

The effects of white privilege were readily apparent in a
room full of white people who needed to be reminded that a
person of color is real, normal, and indeed a person. I
immediately became ashamed that the overwhelming
whiteness of the room made him feel "unreal" and, therefore,
suggested to him that he did not belong.

As a society, we have a tendency to view someone as being
"like" someone else in order to normalize them and explain
why they belong. I have heard white people tell people of
color, "I always just think of you as a white person," as though
it is a compliment. I have heard people say to individuals with
disabilities, "I always forget that you're disabled because you
seem normal to me." In a society that does not allow everyone
the equal opportunity to participate in the daily life of a
community, we have forgotten that disability is a natural part
of human life. There is also, "You don't seem gay to me," said to
gay and lesbian individuals. What is "gay" supposed to seem
like anyway?

The erasure of a person's diversity removes our culpability in their oppression and it absolves our obligation to make things fair. Rather than acknowledging that every human being inherently belongs within their community, we assign honorary membership to those we do not understand by comparing their diversity attributes to ones we identify with.

In order to be consciously aware of how my biases and behavior impact marginalized groups, I explore my own life experiences for foundations of empathy. As an adoptee, my mind quickly arrives at the phrase we hear so often used to describe adoptee relationships:

"They treat her like she's one of their own."

Or,

"They treat her just like blood."

This concept establishes biology as the exclusive standard for family relationships and family belonging. Since adoptees (in this instance) are not biologically related to their adoptive families, adoptees can only ever belong if someone grants them the status of "passing" as biological. In some families, the racial difference of the transracial adoptee is "overlooked" rather than accepted.

Explaining an adoptee's connection to their adoptive family by comparing it to a biological connection exposes the general discomfort people have with accepting and understanding the diversity of adoption. Rather than acknowledging my membership within two distinct family systems, it is easier for someone who is not adopted to push my connections through their biologically-raised lens. In their appraisal of my relationships, they erase not only my existence within my original biological family, but make sense of my adoptive kinship by pretending I was born to a family into which I was not actually born.

The fact that I do belong within my adoptive family without a biological connection suggests that there is an issue with the way that "belonging" is framed. My family should not be required to pretend I am something that I am not in order to say that I belong. No amount of pretending will ever change the fact that I am not their blood kin. The way to change how we think about adoptee belonging is as simple about changing the way that we speak about it. Rather than saying, "I am like one of their own," we can say, "I am their own." We should validate that biology makes us belong, but it is not the only way that we belong. We should let each emotional unit called "family" self-identify their own connections and memberships. The reality is that my parents never loved me like I was someone else. They simply love me for me.

Other People's Parents
Fantastic adoptive parenting doesn't change the lessons other parents teach their kids

While enjoying a friendly chat between mothers in the kitchen of a friend's home, I drifted back to the playroom where several children were sharing toys. A tangle of two boys, one of which was mine, arrived at my feet. The other little boy was sitting on my son's back and pulling his hair. "Boys will be boys," the child's mother replied as she shrugged and walked away.

My son's confused look signified the collision of parenting philosophies. The mother of the little boy thought that boys should roughhouse and work things out on their own. My son has been taught that being a boy does not excuse aggression and that he should not touch someone when they do not want to be touched. I wondered how I would even begin to explain to a three-year-old that it is not OK for him to hurt other children when other parents will stand by while their children hurt him. In that moment, I realized that other people's parenting styles will always be part of the equation in my parenting.

I am reminded of the very common response to adoptee issues, "Your parents must have made all sorts of mistakes." Searching and reunited adoptees hear this. The assumption being that their parents must not have been enough for them that they needed to go out and find another family. Adoptees with grief issues hear that their parents did not raise them "right" or else being adopted would not cause them pain. Adoptees with political platforms hear this. If their parents had done a better job, they would not be seeking to change or improve the adoption system. I think of the little boy who pulled my son's hair and reflect on the peers who figuratively pulled my hair, so to speak, when it came to being adopted. What about other people's parents?

When I was in fifth grade, I attempted to hang my coat at the same time and on the same hook as a classmate. Annoyed at me, this peer decided that my uncouth behavior was the result of being adopted.

"Typical behavior you would expect of an orphan," she sneered at me.

Experiencing this made me realize the possibility that some of my peers did not understand or respect me because I was adopted. It had only taken a moment of anger for a classmate to express a hurtful opinion and bias she harbored about me. I grieved being adopted in that moment.

I was in sixth grade the next time my adoption was used to insult me. My private, conservative Christian school embraced abstinence-only education. Sex before marriage was shameful and made you impure. I knew I was the product of such impurity. One day a classmate decided to point out this fact, suggesting that my mother's supposed promiscuity was genetic and that I would grow up to be "just like her." I was not aware of my conception circumstances at the time. We had been taught that having sex made you promiscuous. I had nothing to defend myself with but to disrupt the classroom by yelling at him angrily. I was punished. My classmate was not.

I grieved being adopted on that day, too.

My parents were never able to talk to the teachers or other parents about these two incidents because I never told my parents it happened. I always had a difficult time telling adults when other peers were unkind to me because I felt embarrassed. I felt like I was admitting that I could not figure out how to be likeable enough on my own for other children not to treat me that way.

Who explained adoption to my peers? My adoptive parents told me that I was chosen and special. So, I tried to think of myself this way. These two peers did not think of me as chosen or special, but rather as something that someone bad had discarded. What had their parents taught them about adoption? Perhaps they were not taught anything at all; the messages about adoption and pregnancy in the surrounding world and media put those unkind ideas into their thoughts.

We need to finally depart from the idea that really great adoptive parents are all an adoptee needs. We need to acknowledge the obligation our communities have to meet our needs for acceptance, respect, and a safe space to be who we are. In point of fact, a great deal of the grief I have experienced is the result of the societal shame associated with being adopted. It is painful to be seen as unwanted, almost aborted,

33

and needing to be grateful just because I am adopted. No amount of perfect parenting on my parents' part could protect me from these cruel assertions. These were issues with other people's parents and the negative messages that other people do not stop from being passed on from generation to generation. If people want to excuse themselves from hearing and understanding an adoptee's grief, they must take responsibility for ending social sources of grief and work to end negative messages about adoptee

The Adoptee Candle
Who do you carry a candle for?

There is something unspeakably beautiful about a simple lit candle. My wedding unity candle is one of my most treasured possessions. I wish I had known my original mother when I got married so that she and my adoptive mother could have lit that flame of life and love together. I often feel an urge to light candles in honor of concerns, struggling loved ones, and painful memories. In situations where I feel powerless, holding vigil in the quiet of my home watching a simple flame wisp around a wick gives me a cosmic sense that I am somehow making a difference. Whenever I am concerned about something or someone, I have the urge to light a candle. With small children in my home, I do not do much keeping of candles these days. Instead, I carry my concerns and joys in a cluster of candles in my heart.

As both a mother and a daughter, I theorize that every baby holds a candle in his or her heart for their mother and a mother for her child. It is the inexplicable symbolic connection between the mother and the child. Biological ties and DNA aside, the connection persists – the burning desire to know the mother or child you briefly knew and lost.

In modern adoption's recent past, it was believed best to try and keep the wicks of these candles from igniting. Infants were removed from mothers as soon after birth as possible. Mothers were denied time to hold their infants. Some mothers awoke after delivery and found themselves no longer on the maternity floor where they might hear the cries of their baby.

For me and for my original mother, our candles stayed lit. I was psychologically present in my original household. My original mother was always, somehow, psychologically present with me. She was the unknown – a myth and fairytale. On some level, though, I knew she was real and that she was mine.

When I have left candles unattended, the watery wax wells up around the wick that threatens to extinguish the flame. Closed adoption made it hard to attend my candle. It was exhausting to try and think about a mother I thought I would never know. The more I thought about being adopted, the more questions I developed that I could not answer.

The days when being adopted was hard, manifesting like bumps in the road, threatened to splash the welled wax over my candle's flame. Still my candle burned.

There were times when my candle burned more brightly than others. I always tried to push thoughts about my original family out of my mind because it was too painful to think about people I thought I would never get to know. Events like my high school graduation, my first big health scare, and the birth of my first child brought the mystery of my origins to consciousness whether I liked it or not.

My candle's flame blazed at the birth of my first son. I finally realized that the flame I carried inside of me for my son was the same as the one I had carried for my original mother. I wondered if she carried a candle for me or if it had gone out.

The expectation of adoption, which makes reunion more difficult, is that adoptive mother replaces the original mother. Do I blow out the candle I have for my adoptive mother in order to reunite with my original mother? The fact of the matter remains; neither mother replaces the other, and there is room in my heart for more than one candle.

Have you ever noticed how candles that are unattended often become covered in layers of built up wax? I think about all of the assumptions I had made about my original family that I had developed growing up as a way of understanding why I was adopted. I had plenty of jagged wax surrounding my candle by the time I reunited. I had to work at removing the wax. Learning to trust and allow myself to feel – and believe it or not, this was something I had to learn when it came to reunion.

I am saddened by the great number of adoptees who were rejected by their original mothers, and vice versa, at reunion. The candle wax has built up, the flame has gone out, and the idea of chipping it all away to leave the wick exposed again is painful. I do not know what it is that keeps the candle's flame going for some mothers and adoptees but not for others. For some, perhaps it is only hope keeping the flame alive – it is a hope that the missing relatives will one day meet again. Perhaps for others, maintaining hope of being found or finding relatives that were lost is too painful or exhausting. The worst thing we can do is to ignore the candles that may be burning bright, dwindling, or flickering in the parents, sons, and daughters around us. The person that we may carry a candle for may not be in our lives, but those who are present with us must hold our feelings and candles dear, offering us love and support.

"Making the decision to have a child is momentous. It is to decide forever to have your heart go walking around outside your body." – Elizabeth Stone

The Fear of Rejection
And how I let it go

"I love you," he said.

"I love you too," I replied.

"I will love you forever," he promised.

"Do not tell me that you love me," my tone was harsh. "Just promise you won't ever leave."

To this day I wonder if my words stung my husband then as badly as they sting me now when I reflect back on this memory.

My husband and I are ideal partners for each other. We risked never having this good relationship because we did not meet at an ideal time. As I got to know him after we first met, I was emotionally torn in two by the realization that he was the right person for me and the awareness that I shouldn't have been dating anyone at that time. I was a young woman, about to embark on my first college experience. He was a young man, finishing up college and about to enter into his career. I had just emerged out of a bad relationship which had tainted my view of relationships and the world in general. I did not know myself very well, who I wanted to be, or what place I felt was mine in the world.

Worse yet, I struggled with lifelong abandonment issues, which left people in my life scrambling to prove that they love me when they had done nothing to warrant distrust in the first place. Fear of being rejected had odd and seemingly opposing effects on my relationships with others. At times, I resisted engaging in positive relationships to avoid feeling hurt if I was rejected later. Other times, I was too eager to be in relationships that were unhealthy, and did not walk away when I should have, because I didn't want to experience rejection—or to cause another person to experience it either.

When I began reading books and literature written by other adult adoptees, I realized that the fear of rejection, although not experienced by every adoptee, is common in the adoptee community. My agency narrative, a one-paragraph abstract of the first chapter of my life, had told me that I wasn't wanted by my original family. I had to come to terms with what it meant to not be wanted by a family. Additionally, what it meant to be "unwanted" by a family that I could not talk to in order to develop a deeper understanding of what occurred before I was adopted. This specific type of loss was intensified by bullying later in my elementary years.

I can only imagine the self-fulfilling prophecy this fear of rejection brought into my life. Acting like every relationship is doomed most certainly doomed some of the friendships and relationships that I had. Rejecting people before they had a chance to reject me limited my networks and support systems growing up. Harboring the fear itself is exhausting.

My fear of rejection was never greater than when I utilized my birth state's confidential intermediary to find my original family and waited for the intermediary to process my request for nearly seven months. The constant worry of what my mailbox might hold each day took an indescribable toll on my emotions.

There came a day when I finally said to myself, "enough." This fear stops now. I realized that I must begin to acknowledge that I am entitled to take up space in this world. I am worthy of being heard. I am deserving of respect, love, and support. I have every right to seek out opportunities and relationships without expecting to feel hurt as a result.

I also began to acknowledge that people make mistakes. Rejection in life is inevitable, but it does not have to be devastating. When I look back on my narrative where I assumed that I was unwanted by my original family, when friends disappointed me, or when bullies harmed my self-esteem, I can either give myself reasons to feel jaded or I can give myself credit for what I've overcome. I can allow memories of feeling rejection to destroy me or I can acknowledge that these experiences have given me survival skills. Yes, rejection is a part of life and yes, it is immensely painful. But I have survived it. I have always survived it and therefore, I know that I always will.

My quest toward self-affirming goals—to love, be loved, be accepted, and take those risks that bring me more reward than pain—has absolutely eased this fear of rejection over time. I have realized that healing starts with me and I am worth so much more than worry about being rejected. The people in my life are worthy of being given a chance to benefit from having me around. I am worthy of being strengthened and benefitted by other people. In the end, when I weigh the risk of rejection against the benefit of accepting the love and support of other people, it's people who win out every single time.

Ungrateful
Who is entitled to my gratitude?

Have you ever seen an adoptee bristle, or felt yourself as an adoptee prickle, when someone mentions that adoptees need to be "grateful?" Where does this reaction come from, and what's wrong with being "grateful" anyway? Gratitude is a wonderful attitude to have for life and blessings in general. However, there's a distinct and unfortunate stereotype of "gratefulness" that adoptees tend to encounter. It's an unhealthy expectation. Here's what you need to know to stop it in its tracks.

The gratefulness seen in family systems causes one generation to look with fondness and care on the previous generation, if they were well cared for by that generation. The adoption-stereotype-gratefulness takes this to an extreme. It expects adoptees to leave things behind so as not to upset some invisible apple cart people imagine adoptive parents to have. What we may be expected to leave behind are our original families, original identity, a quest for reunion or original documentation, or mention of any personal feelings of loss in adoption.

This is an unrealistic gratefulness that is directed at adoptees, and their families, often in an unkind way. In reality, adoptive parents, like all parents, shouldn't want their kids to put aside what may be important to them. It is the job of every parent to nurture the interests, feelings, and ideas of their children. No person, adopted or not, needs to be any more grateful than anyone else for their parents doing what parents are supposed to do. When my adopted identity within my adoptive family exclusively indicates that I need to be grateful, and that gratefulness determines what can and cannot be important to me, I've been made out to be a little less human than everyone else.

I am grateful every day to be the mother of my biologically-raised sons. I do not want a different standard held to me and all of my parents because I am adopted. My sons are entitled to my gratitude for the opportunity to be their mother, but I am not entitled to their gratefulness in return. We need to stop holding to a different standard of gratitude for adoptive families and adoptees because "less than human" isn't a message we want to send.

"I Wish I Were Adopted"
What do people mean when they say this to adoptees?

You've probably heard someone say this, "I wish I was adopted!" It was said mostly in high school during times where teenaged friends just didn't feel like their parents "got" them. They viewed their parents' expectations of them as biologically-based. Their mother or father must want them to get good grades, join the track team, and stop talking on the phone late at night because that's how they're wired and they assume that's how their son or daughter is wired, too. These peers saw being adopted as an opportunity to be a free and unique individual in the midst of genetic strangers who would just embrace whoever you are. It was an opportunity to be a blank canvas and invent oneself. Maybe they didn't realize that my adoptive parents held the same expectations for me. Yep, my adoptive parents still made me pay for my cell phone bill when I went over my minutes. I had to get up on time for school too -- even though I'm adopted.

Family Romance Theory would say that my friends' fantasies about being adopted were part of their development. According to neurologist and founder of psychoanalysis Sigmund Freud, in order to develop identity in adolescence one must compare their parents' values with their own personal values and decide what parts they'll accept as a part of who they are. A teenager might fantasize that they are adopted thinking that their imaginary rock star first parents somewhere out there would "get" them so much better than their actual parents do.

Of course, there is no such fantasy for the adoptee. When an adoptee wonders if they have another set of parents out there who might "get" them better than their adoptive parents do, they are not wondering about fictitious parents. Whether an adoptee has rock star first parents or not, they are not imaginary, they are real. They are real people who, depending on the level of openness in adoption, the adoptee may only be able to create fantasies about because they can't do anything else.

When my peers said things like this, they used their concept of being adopted to say that they think it's easy to be me. To them, at least in that moment, being adopted was what defined me and my entire life. Since they viewed adoption as a positive escape from things in their own lives they did not like, it seemed perfectly acceptable to them to say they wished they could be adopted.

I have a lot of privileges in life, but I don't think it's easy to be me. I don't think it's easy to be anyone.

Yes, their words were insensitive, but not just because they ignored the complexities of being adopted. The insensitivity lies within the assumption that it is easy to be anyone. Everyone has different challenges, some greater and some smaller. Everyone has different resources, strengths, resiliencies, and coping skills. Everyone also has struggles. Some people's challenges are far greater than others. However, saying "I wish I could be you" in some form or another basically sends the message "you don't face challenges" or "the challenges you face aren't important."

The "I wish I could have been adopted" phrase in this context probably would not bother me so much if adoption was not such a complex and highly personal life experience. While one might muse about being adopted during a time of temporary troubles, there are kids waiting in foster care who do actually need to be adopted. Adoption is not a lighthearted matter, rather something that impacts each person differently depending on the circumstances in their life.

Several times in my life, I've made the mistake of believing it would be easier to be someone else. On days that I have sat at home covered in baby food and elbow deep in diapers, I've imagined my friends at their glamorous careers and shopping outings. Each time, it has been a sobering reality when I later discover the hidden struggles they've carried with them that I could not see. When people, not just teenagers, say "OMG, I wish I could be adopted", "I wish I could be you", or "I'd gladly trade my problems for yours!" in other instances, what they most likely mean is "I have a struggle in my life that I wish wasn't there." It's probably best to just say that instead.

In Defense of Reunion
Why you shouldn't assume you know why an adoptee decided to search or reunite

Mary was excited about her Gotcha Day each year. Gotcha Day is the day when adoptions are finalized, or for some adoptees, when they entered into the home of their adoptive parents. Mary's Gotcha Day was like a second birthday, full of excitement and love. Mary's fondness of her Gotcha Day was something I just could not identify with when she explained it to me. I did not like my Gotcha Day. The year I was old enough to realize I had a special day in my family that acknowledged my adoption, I stated my preference not to observe it. Even when a trip to the aquarium was arranged in the day's honor, I asked not to go. "I have a birthday," I told my adoptive mother. And that was that.

After reading this brief glimpse into the life stories of Mary and me, I wonder what people might assume about us and our experiences that led to our views on Gotcha Day. It would be one of many assumptions people make when they encounter adoption and adoptee stories every day.

Surprisingly enough, Mary and I both describe our childhood view of being adopted in the same way. We were both "okay with being adopted." We are about the same age. We were both adopted as infants. We were both raised in loving and supportive adoptive families. As adults, we both acknowledge the complexities of being adopted.

Our similar childhood conclusion on being adopted was simply expressed in different ways. Mary embraced her Gotcha Day because she was okay with being adopted. She wanted to celebrate the special day that made her a part of her adoptive family. I did not want to celebrate my Gotcha Day because I, too, was okay with being adopted. My Gotcha Day reminded me that there was a time when I did not belong in my current family. This was a time I knew nothing about and thought I never would know anything about. My Gotcha Day reminded me that I was different, and I did not feel like being different.

44

Reunited and searching adoptees also encounter assumptions about their quest to meet original family members. I thought I would share the top four reasons why I chose to search and reunite.

I had more love to give to everyone.

I did not reunite to "replace" my parents.

Every human being has dignity and worth as a person; every person in my life has their own unique place. No human being replaces another. Human interaction benefits people and the more connections that I have, the more I benefit those in my life, and they benefit from me in return. Not every connection is perfect and I never expected my connections with my original family to be perfect – just real. I would never have had a chance to know how positive a connection I could have with my original family if I did not seek it out.

I sought an inclusive definition of "family."

I did not reunite because I believe that only biology makes a family.

Biology is one of many elements of family connections. I once had a social connection with my biological family and I sought to restore that. A lot of people think of biological, social, legal, and emotional ties as being embodied all in the same people. Because this is not my reality, choosing to define family by one type of connection but not another would exclude quite a few people whom I care about.

I believed she deserved to know.

I did not reunite to "disrupt" her life or because I felt she "owed" me something.

I never planned to think about being adopted when I gave birth to my first child. It simply happened, and it hit me like a ton of bricks. I looked at my sweet little boy and I could not imagine never knowing anything about him or not seeing him again. Yet, my mother had lived almost 25 years without knowing who or where her child was. Connecting this fact to

45

my own motherhood sent a sense of terrible grief through every part of my heart and soul.

I accepted that my original mother might not want to know me. But I believed that she deserved the chance to make that choice herself.

I believed that my kids deserved to know.

I did not reunite because I was ungrateful for the blessings in my life.

The day I chose to become a parent was the day that I became an advocate for the precious lives that I brought into the world. The reality of being an adoptee with sealed records is that, in some states, only the adoptee can open them. Often times, successful search, reunion, and genealogy gathering is not helped at all by accessing records. These aspects are helped instead by interviewing relatives and other people connected to both your adoptive and original families and following up on information provided. The more generations that pass, the more memories there are to provide clues regarding what was lost.

I realized from having a father whose own mother is adopted that my refusal to access my roots would mean that my children could not access half of their own roots either. To go without half of their roots is a choice that I did not feel that I had a right to make for them.

Perhaps the most bizarre assumption people have is that searching and reunited adoptees believe that they will find blissfully perfect human relationships at the end of their search. Adoptees, like everyone else, experience challenges and triumphs in life. We are aware that human relationships are not perfect. I sought reunion and I found it. I cherish the family I found each and every day. Yet my story is just a drop in an ocean full of many other reunion stories.

When we assume that from one piece of information, whether it is how someone feels about Gotcha Day or that they would like to reunite, that we know everything about their beliefs and experiences in adoption, we lose out on what could be learned. Assumptions make every adoptee the same. The assumed story plays over and over again in our minds and we lose compassion for the individuals and their family systems. Let adoptees give meaning to their story. Your assumptions

about them say more about your own biases than they do
about the real story.

Should I be Glad to be Adopted?
A question that doesn't have a definitive answer for me

I was dining with a friend one afternoon. In between bites of hand-cut fries dashed with tasty sea salt, I regaled her with the experience of unsealing my adoption files, finding my original family, and reuniting. As a mother who surrendered her son to adoption in the 1970s, she was interested to know how I was processing all of this new information. We talked about what it was like to go from having a short agency narrative to understanding a much larger picture of my story. Then she hit me with it, that question I do not think any adoptee wants to be asked. She wanted to know if I felt glad to be adopted.

This may seem like a strange time to be having a conversation like this, in a noisy restaurant, talking between bites of free-range bison sliders and baked kettle chips. But it was a safe environment. I was with a friend whom I knew would understand me and who would let me talk this important concept out.

The answer to such a question is very easy to misunderstand. If an adoptee says that he is not glad to have been adopted, this may sound like he is saying "I wish I never knew you" to their adoptive family. On the other hand, if an adoptee says that she is glad to have been adopted, this may sound like she is saying "I am glad I was not raised by you" to her original family.

I think it is understandable for other people to inquire about the meaning an adoptee has assigned to adoption in their life after they have experienced reunion. However, part of asking such an intense and deeply personal question is being open to the answer. This includes not insisting that how an adoptee feels about being adopted must be filed into one of two categories: "I wish I was" or "I wish I was not."

There is some trouble with being asked to compare two lives in this way. One life was never lived and exists only through imagination and guessing games. The other life is filled with memories, lived experiences, and concrete places. One life is a fantasy that could have been and the other life is home.

We should take care not to ignore the difficult task adoptees have of integrating two selves, two realities, and two families. The fact of the matter is that the positives and negatives of my adoption are so interwoven that they are impossible to separate into any sort of neat category.

I love my adoptive family, and I do not regret being raised by them. I realize that I came to them after their long and painful bout with infertility. Without their infertility, I would not have become a member of the family. I love that they are my family, but if by some cosmic blessing I had the power, I would take their infertility and the subsequent grief and loss away.

I love my original family, and I do not think they would have done a bad job raising me. I realize that surrendering me to adoption was extremely painful for them, especially my mother. It was through my original mother's grief and loss that my adoptive parents were able to become parents. While I do not regret being raised by my adoptive parents, if by some cosmic blessing I had the power, I would never wish the loss of a child to adoption on my original family.

Wishing my adoptive parents had never been infertile and wishing that my original family had never experienced the loss of a family member is not about regretting being adopted. It simply comes from a place of love. Part of loving both of my families is wishing that they never had pain, even if those wishes do not fall neatly and logically into my life's storyline.

Thus far, I have made a great case as to why it simply does not make sense to ask adoptees if they are glad to have been adopted. On a deeper level, I am glad that my friend's question caused me to explore how I feel about being adopted on a deeper level. I did not expect to make a simple, definitive "yes" or "no" conclusion. I simply gave myself the opportunity to assign greater meaning to being adopted. The question transformed into: "What do I decide about the story of my life?" The meaning I give to my adoption is not wishing that it did or did not happen. I will never be able to come to either of those conclusions. I have decided that adoption in my life presents both strengths and challenges along with joys and heartaches. What this means to me is that I have a lifetime to love and be loved by a lot of people.

How not to Shut Down Adoption Discourse
And how to ask someone about their family

Those of us connected to adoption get asked some pretty intense questions from family members, friends, co-workers, and random strangers. In fact, one of the most frequently discussed topics in the larger adoption community is the "Things People Ask That They Shouldn't" variety. The answers to the questions run the gamut from snark, to serious answers, and to light-hearted replies. More often than not, the responses send the message that people should feel badly for asking and that they should not ask about adoption. Perhaps even that they should ignore adoption. It is not OK to ask anything. However, is shutting down adoption discourse what we really want?

It is true that many of the questions those of us connected to adoption get asked are presumptive, too personal, or even unkind. Perhaps unintentionally so. This essay will not tell the adoption community how to deal with the questions or overlook what makes them uncomfortable about certain adoption-related questions. I want to appeal to those who may someday ask an adoptee a question to do so in a way that is respectful. I will cover adoptee-focused questions, although comparable questions may get asked of other adoption community members.

The hallmark of inappropriate questions is that they are filled with micro-aggressions -- underlying messages that get sent along with the question. Micro-aggressions reflect biases and often are not what you meant to say at all.

Good questions are strengths-first, person-first. Meaning they consider the feelings of the person answering a question first above the necessity for information. It also means that the questions hold any human being spoken about in positive regard. It does not mean you tell another person, "This given thing in your life is wonderful." Only she can give elements of her own narrative meaning. It means you imply, "You are wonderful. You have value to me."

"Where are your real parents?"

Usually when someone asks this, they mean an adoptee's biological parents. Sometimes people say "real parents" to mean the adoptive parents. I always tell people, "All of my parents are real," because that is how I identify. If you are going to use a label for someone's parents, you should ask them what words he uses first, and then refer to his relatives the way that he does: "How would you like for me to refer to your parents?" And instead of asking, "Where are they?" (which assumes an adoptee knows where her parents are), ask, "Have you met them?"

"Couldn't your parents have their own kids?"

This question assigns "their own" to biology and "like their own" to being adopted. The underlying a message that an adoptee may receive is: "You're not their own." It is important to validate an adoptee's membership within all of the families that she identifies with. If you want to know if an adoptee's adoptive parents struggled with infertility why not ask just that? Or ask, "Do you know why your parents adopted?"

"Are your adoptive parents angry you reunited?"

Reunion is something that not all adoptive parents are supportive of. However, this question assumes that this is the response that all adoptive parents have or should have. It also potentially sends the message that the adoptee did something wrong by seeking reunion, which makes it likely his parents would be angry. Remember, person-first, strengths-first. Why not just say, "What was your parents reaction?" or "How have your parents supported you through this?"

"Was your birth mother on drugs?"

A question phrased like this is based on the bias that most original mothers were doing drugs when their children were adopted. Therefore, it is safe to phrase a question that frames any given adoptee's original mother the same way. In reality, research shows us that drugs are just a small part of why

51

children end up in foster care and even a smaller element of private adoptions. Strengths-first, person-first. Why not just ask, "Can you tell me what you know about her?"

"I bet you feel ____."

These are not so much questions as they are phrases. There are times when these statements are okay and times when they are not. When phrases like these are issued before adoptees says how they feel, the phrases assign meaning to the adoptees' experience on behalf of the adoptees, based on the speaker's own ideas of adoption. Be more eager to really listen to the answer rather than eager to respond to it.

These phrases are useful when you have already listened to someone assign meaning to their own story. It is called reflective responding: "You said this made you happy; I am glad to hear that." or, " I understand this was hard for you; I am really sorry about that."

Before asking a person anything that is potentially very personal, it is polite to ask: "Is it okay if I ask you about this?" or "Are any topics off-limits for you?" If you feel uncomfortable or "too serious" prefacing your questions/discussion this way, consider that the questions might not be appropriate for your relationship type, level of intimacy, or the setting you are in. Perhaps you should not be asking at all. Remember that questions should be asked when it is relevant and helpful to the person you are talking to and to the larger community. Be genuine, be empathetic, and be intentional.

Part Two: Living Adoption

"Adult adoptees are a primary source for knowledge about adoption as an institution. Their perceptions are unique, for adult adoptees are actually the only persons who can tell us what it is like to live adoption in a society in which most people are not adopted." – Child Welfare League of America

A Letter to my Prospective Adoptive Mother
What that little baby might have wanted to say

To my prospective adoptive mother,

It is 1985. My name is Christen, but here they call me "Sarah." I was three days old when I last saw my first mother and was placed in foster care. I have been here for almost five months. I do not know why. I have a foster mother. I do not know her name.

You drove from Georgia to Tennessee to see me. You were apprehensive holding me. They warned you before coming in that I cry relentlessly for everyone who has considered adopting me into their family. You breathe a sigh of relief because I do not cry when you pick me up. Now, 20 minutes have passed since you have been holding me and I am still quietly gazing up at you. You will be my third mom. You will be my last mom.

You ask how to best raise an adopted child and the experts tell you that I have no unique needs and that being adopted, though you should disclose it to me as soon as possible, will mean nothing to me. They will give you no post-adoption support. But we are strong.

We will have so much fun when I am little. We will move to the East Coast near the ocean. I will follow you and want to do everything that you do. I will exhibit talent for language and music and you will do your best to nurture it. We will go to the beach every day in the summer. You will watch me sit by the shore for hours on end, but you will not know that I am wondering why I feel so drawn to the ocean if my original family is from Tennessee. Times will be hard. Money will be tight until daddy's business takes off when I am a teenager. But we will be fine.

My elementary school years will be hard for all of us. I will be head strong, smart, and have a style of my own. The other children will make fun of me. You will dry my tears every night from 4th grade until 6th grade. You will reprimand my teachers. You will write stern letters to the apathetic school administration. You will feel like you have done nothing while

54

doing absolutely everything. I will tell you that you are not my "real mom" a handful of times out of frustration and not feeling understood by others. You, a naturally quiet and demure person, will watch your daughter develop a quick wit and sharp tongue. I will test you, I will push your buttons, and I will make you prove over and over again that you love me.

You will watch me blossom into a teenager who will get good grades, and become captain of the basketball team and rapidly popular with many friends. You will drive my friends and me everywhere and you will love them. You will be frustrated when I spend too much energy on people who do not care about me because I will not be able to stand rejecting anyone. When I teeter on the brink of adulthood in a relationship that is not healthy for me, you will feel like you do not know what to do. It will be one of only two times that you will see your husband cry.

I will ditch my uncaring boyfriend and embark on a long process of self-discovery and finding what I want to do as a career. You will light my unity candle at my wedding where you will invite nearly everyone you have ever met to share your proud moment. Then, with no family medical history, I will discover a tumor. I will cry for you sick from pain and anesthesia when I wake up from the surgery. You will ask God "why" and I will be okay.

You will be there for the birth of your first grandchild and watch me blossom into a mother. You will watch the adoptee in me awaken. You will be bewildered when I start talking about being adopted, missing my first mother, and my interest in my roots. You will cry tears of frustration at the dormant pain that suddenly erupts from my soul. You will not understand my delight to find out that long have my ancestors lived near the ocean. When I embark on reunion, you will support me, but feel as though I am rejecting you. I will have to tell you over and over again that I am not leaving you, but regaining part of me that was left behind. You will meet the mother who shares your daughter. You will give her pictures of my childhood. You will see her face and hold her in your arms. You will watch your daughter give meaning to loss and turn it into good in a career that helps others. You will watch her genetic traits and personality and the values and skills you taught her put to action. You will come with me to Adoptee Rights events. You will not understand why at first, but you will want to, and eventually, you will understand the movement. You will become one of my best friends and greatest allies.

And you will finally know that you are a good mother.

Welcome to motherhood.

Are you ready?

Love,
The Baby You Hold in Your Arms

Misidentified Jealousy in Reunion
How love can conquer insecurity when families reconnect

I have lost track of how many times people have asked me what my parents think about my reunion. Some of the questions are quite specific, such as, "How did your adoptive mother handle your reunion? How did it make her feel?" People ask these questions for many reasons. Fellow adoptees may be trying to gauge how their own adoptive parents might react if they revealed the "I'm searching" news. Others may be curious for less innocent reasons. People tend to think of adoption exclusively as a service to build families for adoptive parents. With this mindset, adoptee reunions may be perceived as disloyal to the adoptive family for identifying outside of the adoptive family system. They picture the adoptees toppling over a neatly stacked apple cart that the adoptive parents worked hard to establish, with apples chaotically scattering on the ground. Regardless of why someone wants to know, it is true that adoptees reunions can be very emotional times for their adoptive parents.

Over the years, I have met adoptees whose adoptive parents vary in their level of support for search and reunion. One friend's mother helped facilitate her reunion and was so involved you would have thought she had found her own mother. I have another friend whose adoptive parents stopped speaking to her after she reunited. Yet another friend had her adoptive parents' blessing to search, but they have forbidden her to speak of it.

My parents were somewhere in the middle. They accepted my search, but my reunion was initially hard for them. They sought out ways to become more supportive while respecting my space as an adult.

I was adopted during the tail end of a modern adoption era where most private infant, agency-facilitated domestic adoptions were closed. It was still common in adoption practice to make adoptive families appear as close as possible to biological families. According to my file, my agency matched me with my parents because they thought our features were similar enough to pass as biological kin. I was, as the law says, "As if born to." My parents were told that while I may have some questions about my adoption, we would be exactly like all other families. This was the extent of the post-adoption support they received. There was certainly no preparation for possible future reunion.

Despite growing up in a loving and supportive environment, announcing my reunion to my adoptive parents was still very hard. I anticipated that my search might hurt their feelings. I did not talk about being adopted very frequently when I was growing up. I knew this was going to be coming out of nowhere for them.

When I finally decided to actively take the steps toward finding and reunion, I felt like I needed my adoptive parents' blessing. If they had withheld, that would not have stopped me from searching. However, I sought reassurance that I was not going to be alone. This is why I needed my husband's support, too.

When I first told my adoptive mother that I wanted to search, she confided in me that she had anticipated that the day would come. I do not think any amount of anticipation prepared her to deal with feelings of being replaced. She feared losing her place as my mother and as a grandmother to my children.

My adoptive mother tentatively accepted the news of my search, and requested that I keep her updated on my progress. When I would share details of my search progress with her, I could feel the hurt and stress emanate from her. When I did not share things with her, she felt left out. It developed into a painful catch-22.

One day, she asked me to consciously explore her experience of having an adopted daughter who was searching for her original mother. I had recently become a mother to my oldest son.

"Amanda, what if your son, all of a sudden wanted to go search for another mom out there?" she wanted to know. "How would you feel if you had to share him?"

I did stop for a minute to imagine how hard it might be to not be the only mother in my son's life. My gut reaction was to feel an emotion that was overwhelming to me. What was it? Jealousy? Fear? Defensiveness? I imagined that feeling like I shared my son with another might be hard, if I chose to approach the relationship that way. On the other hand, this is what stepmothers, mothers in very open adoptions, and mothers in same-sex relationships make expert work of everyday of their lives, right?

58

I realized that part of the hardship between us in the search and reunion matter was how the role of mother was being framed.

This was my reply. "My son is not adopted. I am. He does not have another mother out there. I do. I suppose that if I had adopted my son, I would have to acknowledge that he does have another mother and anticipate the fact that he would also see her as mother and want to know her. I would not expect him to deny what is important to him and part of him in order to support my feelings. That wouldn't be fair."

In the end, my adoptive mother's gut reaction to my reunion was not her fault or anything that she could initially help. At the time of my adoption, adoption policy and practice set up with the expectation that the adoptive parents replace the original parents in every way imaginable.

It would have been wrong for my adoptive mother never to move past that gut reaction. It would have been wrong for me to never move past the hurt I felt in response to her gut reaction. When the adoptive family and original family do not know each other, this reality breeds fear. The status of my original mother as mere myth was quickly dispelled when my adoptive mother was able to see her. She discovered that my original mother was not an enemy who sought to take her place, but a real person with vulnerabilities and fears of her own.

I do not know that the fears and insecurities, what may be mistaken as jealousy, ever completely go away. However, as time goes on, understanding each other's feelings and intentions has become easier.

The searching adoptee embarks on a journey that can be full of unknowns and worries. We do not know if we will find open arms, a door slammed in our faces, or even a grave. We may have religions, worldviews, political ideas, cultural practices, and languages that differ from those of our original families. We may fear that, even if a connection can be made, we have too little in common to carry on a relationship. The fear of rejection is compounded by the reality that one's adoptive parents may create emotional distance or an emotional cut-off as the result of reunion.

So the question must be asked: "Is search and reunion worth it if an adoptee will lose every connection they have?" Only adoptees can make that determination for themselves.

This is the message that I bring to every person who loves a searching adoptee or one who may one day search. Be aware of the emotional rollercoaster that the unknowns of closed adoption search may present for the adoptee. They may be carrying invisible worries that you cannot see. Remember that search and reunion for a closed adoption adoptee involves uncovering what was buried on our behalf as children. Some of us must unseal the records impounded by the court. Some of us must petition for access to the birth certificates that our birth states never anticipated we would want to see.

Those of us who seek reunion ultimately attempt in some way to reestablish the connection and communication that was severed when we left the care of our original mothers and fathers. Some of us must board planes and visit our states and countries of birth, boldly grasping for the sense that we belong there and are entitled to be there. This requires empowerment rather than trepidation. Adoptive parents have the unique opportunity to be a source of empowerment for the searching adoptee. This is a sacred duty, much like the job of being a parent itself, which cannot be taken lightly.

Adoptive Family Tolerance for Differentiation
Does it predict search and reunion outcomes?

While I was waiting for my birth state's confidential intermediary to clear the way for contact with my original family, one of my friends traced my genealogy for me. For the first time, I held in my hands the names and histories of ancestors who were blood-related. People who no doubt looked like me and could provide some clue to my natural abilities. Excitedly, I told my adoptive mother who was on her own journey trying to accept my sudden quest for my roots and give it meaning in her own life and experience as an adoptive parent. The conversation took place several years ago, but I can still remember it like it was yesterday.

"I am English and Scottish!" I told my adoptive mother excitedly.

"I thought you were whatever we were." Her reply had an apprehensive ring.

I was filled with many emotions at once. There was anger, sadness, shame, defensiveness, remorse, indifference, and some others I cannot describe. My mother perceived my excitement over my biological heritage as a rejection of the family from which she was descended. I was born English and Scottish. I had to leave those things behind in closed adoption. I think for the first time, without realizing it, she felt what it feels like to have an integral piece of who you are rejected. Neither of us, until that moment, realized how important our own biological roots were to us, or how badly it felt to perceive those roots as being insulted.

When I learned about family systems in college, we acknowledged that families can be anywhere on a spectrum from "enmeshed" to "disengaged." When families are enmeshed, they are close and dependent on one another. When families are disengaged, they are more independent from other family members. It is said it is good to be somewhere in the middle, but a family's level of being more enmeshed or disengaged can also be culturally determined.

One variable that makes families more enmeshed or more disengaged is how much differentiation is tolerated for each family member by the overall family system. In other words, differentiation is how comfortable the family system is with members of the family identifying outside the boundaries of the system. Identifying outside of the adoptive family in some way is what adoptees must do in order to search or reunite.

Families have family boundaries in order to identify as an emotional unit. Like in my adoptive family, sometimes these boundaries are more rigid than others. For an example of more rigid boundary, my family held religious beliefs that were important for our family to follow. These beliefs were contained within the boundaries of our family system and were not open to change from outside influences. Closed adoption can be seen as enforcing a rigid boundary in an adoptive family system by automatically excluding the non-present original family from the adoptive family's boundaries. This intensified the difficulty of deciding to search for my original family because it required me to reclaim the identity that I have outside of my adoptive family system.

My intention is not to portray families with more rigid boundaries in a poor light. Some parents had long hard road of personal self-discovery from their own childhoods. When it comes to raising their children, they may view it as important raise a child to embrace their own truths in order to inter-generationally transmit something positive.

With initially rigid rules that defined our family as being exclusive to adoptive family ties, it was hard for all of us when I grabbed hold of my pre-adoption identity and acknowledged my identity within another family system. The possibility of reunion had always resided in my adoptive parents' consciousness, but the fruition of this possibility had always been somewhat outside of their personal lens on life and family. My adoptive mother grew up in a traditional two-parent household. Her parents were married for over 60 years. My father was able to pull from his own childhood and unique situation of not being raised in a traditional home or by his original mother to connect with my experience. His understanding of my thought process when I went to search ultimately strengthened my adoptive family's understanding of my needs and my understanding of their feelings.

When it came time to announce my search and reunion, my perceptions of how I felt my differentiation might be tolerated by my adoptive family became a key part of my fears. Today's most truly open adoptions are ones in which the adoptee and adoptive family have direct contact with the original family while actively maintaining flexibility in the family system. An adoptee identifies as a part of both families and each family has made room for the other. Families of closed adoption in reunion are capable of this as well. We can take our cue from these families who have embraced openness and see how the expansion of connections through openness benefits everyone involved. Each family of closed adoption that establishes openness through reunion may have to step outside of its comfort zone, but each member of the family must understand that they do so in support of the adoptee. In the end, reunion is not just about restoring a connection that was lost. It is about nurturing family relationships for years to come.

Exposing the Secret Sister
How adoption made me the secret I never wanted to be

It was a warm Sunday evening. Darkness had just settled outside. Church-goers filed cheerfully out the swinging double-doors of the sanctuary, barely tripping over children who could not wait to escape sitting still and find freedom outside. I did not budge. My eyes were fixed on the modest bookshelf at the back of the sanctuary. It held pamphlets, free Bibles, and hearing devices for those needing some extra help listening to the service. Eventually, my eyes became fixed on the brightly colored packages at the very top of the faux wood shelf. Actually, most of my interest lied in one package that had not been deposited there yet, my mother's present from her "secret sister."

"Amanda, what in the world are you doing?" my mother inquired.

"Waiting for your secret sister to drop off your gift," I replied matter-of-factly.

"Well, she's not going to leave it there with you staring a hole through the shelf." Her reply was filled with amusement. "It's called 'secret sister' for a reason."

"Fine, I'll figure out who she is another way," I sighed.

"Amanda JoAnn!" She chided, gently. "Don't you think that defeats the purpose?"

"I don't get the purpose. Why would you have a sister who is a secret and who leaves gifts for you?" I responded. "Wouldn't you want to know who your sister is so you could be friends? So she can know what it is you want or would like instead of buying random gifts? It makes no sense to me!"

She sighed and we walked together out of the sanctuary. She was not going to win that argument. Not that day anyway. Nine-year-olds can be very stubborn that way. I was no exception.

I finally did figure out the identity of my mother's "secret sister." Following more careful bookshelf stakeouts, hilariously-amateur psychoanalysis of the types of presents left for my mother, and careful inspection of the hand-written notes that accompanied the packages, I figured out that the "secret sister" was my mother's friend Lila. Out of respect, I did not tell my mother who it was, but I did do a gleeful dance in her presence, taunting gently in a sing-song voice, "I know who it is! I know who it is!" She simply smirked playfully at my delight over this simple discovery, not understanding why this was such a big deal to me.

Why was it such a big deal to me? I am a relatively practical person and perhaps a bit of an idealist. Did the secrecy of the friendship gift-giving game not make sense to me on a matter of practicality? How do you know what someone else wants or needs unless you know who you are and can ask them? Perhaps on some level, I was taking a stand against the secrecy that surrounded parts of my life as a closed-adoption adoptee. I always knew that my original mother was young and that she could very well likely have more children – my brothers and sisters. As someone who was raised an only child, the thought of siblings delighted and bewildered me. Did I have a secret sister?

The answer is no, I never had a secret sister. The reality was that I had three brothers who regarded me as their secret sister. My paternal brother spent the first 24 years of my life, up until the discovery of my first families, considering me to be non-existent. He cannot incorporate me into his life and I accept his decision. My two maternal brothers have always known about me and waited with my mother, year after year, for me to reenter their lives. The agency had presented the adoption as though reunion was something that was always around the corner and so my mother waited for me to be coming around that corner. When my brothers grew old enough to understand, they waited too.

This is what secrecy in adoption did to my family. I waited on one side wondering if I had a family who wanted to know me. My family waited on the other side, eyes fixed on their own faux wood bookshelf of sorts, anticipating their secret sister. I never wanted to be a secret or the source of someone else's anxiety due to my absence. My adoptive parents never wanted that either.

I did not like the secret sister game – it was one I never asked to play.

I Needed Permission to Love her
When memories help you find what you were looking for

"Amanda, you cannot get up there and tell that story," my adoptive mother warned me.

I looked at her, puzzled. This was my story. Why could I not share it?

"That's not how it happened," she said. "I don't know where you got that story from, Amanda."

I was 14-years-old and about to deliver a speech for a pro-life debate at my conservative Christian school. At the time, I still believed in using myself as an example of someone's mother "choosing life." I also believed that my original parents were teenagers who had been irresponsible. Instead of choosing abortion, they chose adoption. As a result of that decision, I was here.

Wait a minute, you mean that is not how it happened?

Over my 14 years of life, I had concocted a story of my pre-adoption narrative to fill in the blanks of what I did not know. I used the common stereotypes of abortion, adoption, and unplanned pregnancy to make sense of the gaps in my narrative. It was not until that moment in my mother's office at my school that I realized that I had done this. In fact, no one had ever told me anything about my biological father until that moment in time. Likewise, I had never asked about him.

Of course, it had not been developmentally appropriate for me to be told about my biological father any sooner than at that moment. My parents had always planned to tell me, but this moment increased the sense of urgency in doing so because my adoptive mother is a very honest person. She could not bear the thought of me getting up there and telling this story that I unintentionally made up. Luckily, she was the secretary of my high school at the time and something urged me to check in with her about my narrative before taking the stage for the debate.

She told me what little she knew about my biological father.

There was not much I could do with that information at that point. I just blankly said "okay" and walked out of her office. I did not have time to be emotional or react because then people would have asked me what was wrong and I did not want to tell them. I quickly adjusted my speech by simply taking out anything where I might have mentioned the word "father" in it and went on about my day. I remember thinking to myself, "Do you want to think about this now? Nope. Okay then." And I went on as if I had never been told.

Post-reunion, I asked my adoptive mother to write down the story of what she remembered of that day. She replied, "One day Amanda came rushing into my office and said, 'Mom, tell me how I was conceived.' I don't remember her exact words, but understood what she needed to know and was in a hurry for the information. I just gave her the quick version from the information I had. I told her that it was a forced relationship and that her birth mother was very young. Her response was, 'We like her, don't we?' I said, 'Yes, we do. I think she was a very brave young woman.' That was about it. She ran off to her class and she never asked about anything more pertaining to her conception or adoption."

I felt shocked by my adoptive mother's recollection of this event. I had completely forgotten the last part. Reading those words that I sad, "We like her, don't we?" sent a rush of old questions and emotions to the forefront of my mind.

At age 14 with little information to go on because of the nature of closed adoption, I was still at a place in my life where I was deciding on how to feel about being adopted. It is hard to decide what is right to think and feel when your questions cannot really be answered in order to do so. What was perhaps even harder for me was the fact that there were other people whom I loved (my adoptive family) involved. I wanted what meaning and feelings I gave to my adoption, of course, never to hurt their feelings. I felt the need to make sense of my adoption; to give meaning to this very real, tangible yet intangible, mystery that surrounded my very existence on this earth.

At that moment in my adoptive mother's office, she was put in the place of having to be very frank with me about an uncomfortable topic. I responded back with a seemingly benign question. Oddly enough, my response had nothing to do with my conception circumstances. The truth was that I had feelings regarding an uncomfortable topic that I was afraid to bring up to my parents.

Can I love my original mother? Would they support me in loving her?

Needing permission to love my original mother was not something imposed on me or implied by anything my parents did or said. Somehow, it became a rule I had made for myself. I suppose it was the most logical choice at the time. I did not know how to feel about being adopted, and it made sense to ask the only other people whom I intimately knew who were themselves connected to adoption. If I felt how they did, no one could get hurt by my feelings. As an adult, it has become liberating to realize that I do not need anyone's permission to love my mother or any other human being on this planet. It is also empowering to know that my adoptive mother supports my ability to establish my own connections and feelings.

Internalizing Adoption Messages
How my parents got it right

"They're letting her come to the social."

I barely heard Leah as her words pulled me from one of my daydreams and back to the picnic bench where we sat.

"What?" I replied to my classmate, with a puzzled look.

Leah rolled her eyes at me. "Avery," she huffed, shifting her weight and adjusting her uncomfortable uniform skirt. "They're letting her go to the social. But she can't sit up front."

My curiosity was piqued. "Why do they care where she sits?"

Leah rolled her eyes at me. "They don't want anyone to see, you know, her stomach."

I let out an annoyed groan.

Avery had to leave our private religious high school earlier that year because she had committed the "ultimate sin" possible for a girl our age.

Avery was pregnant.

Avery had not been kind to me throughout the years we attended school together. When we were in middle school, she relentlessly teased me on the school bus. In high school when I became nearly as popular as she was, Avery smugly pretended that I was invisible. I often wondered if she treated me this way because my existence was simply offensive to her or because I was one of the few girls at school who did not care about what she thought.

As Avery's stomach grew, my indifference to her melted into inexplicable compassion. I felt a strong need to defend her when people gossiped behind her back. I internally railed against the school administration who wanted her to sit in the back of the room at her senior class' party. When the baby's father was lost in a tragic accident while Avery was still pregnant, I went to the funeral and wept bitterly for their tiny almost-family.

When I reached adulthood, I was finally able to understand why my feelings about Avery had changed. As an unmarried, unprepared, and pregnant teenager, Avery fit all of the descriptive factors that had been used to explain why my own first mother could not keep me. Avery, in some small way, became a symbol of my young first mother.

In the end, Avery kept her baby.

I did not realize at the time how deeply intertwined my feelings about myself were with my feelings for my first mother. I saw no difference in how people looked at Avery and how they might have looked at my own mother with her swollen belly. How can someone be ashamed of the beautiful mother without also being ashamed of her beautiful baby? It was clear that people thought Avery should be ashamed. In a way, it made me feel ashamed, too.

My parents ultimately could not keep me from observing how unkindly many people treated others, especially girls like Avery, outside the walls of our home. What matters to me most, though, is that my parents were – and are – kind people. They spoke highly of my first mother, a woman they had never met. They also never uttered a negative judgment about my biological father. I am not sure I will ever be able to fully fathom what a daunting task it must have been for my parents to tell me about my biological father with such a high level of thoughtfulness.

I sometimes tell this story to original parents and adoptive parents who ask me how they should share difficult information with an adopted child. Revisiting this story now forces me to realize that my parents never received advice on how to speak to me about my adoption. My mother once told me, "We told you the details of your pre-adoption story that we knew. We were careful never to speak as though someone you are related to is a horrible person. We wanted you to know the truth without your coming to the conclusion that you are horrible, too." They made a choice and simply hoped it was the right thing to do. I finally made sure to tell them I think they were wise.

Six Ways I Appreciate Biology
Embracing my biological roots post-reunion

When it comes to reunion, some might argue that it is not a biological connection that the adoptee is seeking, but rather a rekindling of the brief social relationship that began early in life. As a reunited adoptee, I have never been able to categorize my reunion and reasoning for reuniting so neatly into two clearly separate parts. At the moment of my birth, my connection to my original mother was comprised of biological, social, and legal ties. Adoption cut off the social and legal ties with my family. Adoption practices at the time attempted to cut the biological ties simply by limiting what I was permitted to know about my biological family. However, adoption did not change my DNA or the fact that I am and always will be the biological relative of my first family.

When I reunited, I sought to re-establish my social connection with my own biological roots. And I have thought of ways in which rekindling the social connection with my biological family has made a difference in my everyday life.

I have stopped trying to beat my hair into submission.

During my teen years, I could never just get a trim whenever I visited the salon. Every haircut was different. I donned both long and short styles. Twice, I went from near-waist-length hair to cutting off an entire ponytail to donate, embracing a new 'do' that sat well above my chin. I also never dyed it the same color more than once. Every time my roots started to grow out, I saw it as an opportunity to reinvent my look. I started dying my hair when I was about 12-years-old and by age 20 could not tell you the tone of my natural hair color.

I have battled with my hair for years trying to get it to look the way that I wanted it to. I had a rule that if I could not blow my hair dry and flat iron it, I would wear it up. When my hair air dried, it would always flip out in the opposite direction that it was cut to fall. It would never look the way the haircut was styled without some serious intervention from the flat iron and some hairspray.

It never occurred to me until reunion that my hair might actually be naturally wavy and might look nice if I cut and styled it using my hair's natural waves. Most of the young women in my maternal family wear their hair long, and wavy. There is nothing like seeing a feature that you have be mirrored by someone else that makes you think, "Wow, that's beautiful."

I warily integrate my family medical history.

I spent a long time ignoring what relevance biology may have in my life. Like it or not, I was not dealt very good cards in the health game. My biological father died from brain cancer when I was eighteen. Almost every ancestor for three generations in my paternal family has had cancer. Both cancer and benign tumors run in my paternal biological family. My paternal aunt was not at all surprised to hear that I had a benign tumor at the age of 21. I am also genetically predisposed to diabetes on both sides of my biological families.

I did not want this to be my family medical history. This is what it is, though, and I need to acknowledge this truth. I need to wisely use this information with my doctors to make health care decisions.

I have become the "rescuer" and "preserver" of heirlooms.

When my husband suggested that he did not want his grandfather's antique pocket watch any longer and was considering giving it to our four-year-old to play with, I all but hit the floor in response. I took the intricately engraved bass piece in my hand and found the spring to pop it open. Inside was a photograph of my husband's great-grandfather as a child. In the photo, he bears a striking resemblance to my oldest son. It is now hidden away with all of my other treasures: old photographs of family members, my grandmother's hairdresser's charm, my grandfather's medal for decades of factory service, my paternal family's china, and my maternal great-grandmother's adoption papers and original birth certificate.

I have created some heirlooms myself. Before I was reunited or even married, I walked into a jewelry store and the most beautiful ring and matching pendent caught my eye. It was a citrine stone enveloped in a circle of tiny diamonds. I immediately thought, "This is what I want to wear at my wedding and pass on to future generations."

My husband's disconnect from the pocket watch heirloom is the result of knowing his grandfather, but never having a strong connection with him personally. I keep this in mind with the traditions that I start and the heirlooms of mine that I save to be passed down. These are not just objects. These are gifts to my descendants, generations of which I will not be around to meet, but helped bring into the world. These items are my way of saying, "This is who I was," "Please remember me," and "Please know I loved you all before you were even born."

I reminisce about memories in new ways.

Some of my fondest memories are ones I like to turn over and over again through new eyes.

When I was in high school, my friends would eagerly gather at my house to have their hair done before a school social or party. We would sit around with curlers in our hair and paint our nails, do horrific amounts of plucking of eyebrows, and convince ourselves that the overpriced mascara really did add volume to our eyelashes. I would set up a chair and style everyone's hair into some outrageous up-do.

Can you imagine how excited I was to learn that my grandmother was a hairstylist and had her own salon? I look back at these memories and wonder how much of my skill at styling my friends' hair was influenced by skills I inherited from her.

I can talk about heredity without having to say "I'm adopted" to make sense.

When I was pregnant with my first son, I cannot tell you how many times people asked me these questions:

How much did you weigh when you were born?

I don't know, I'm adopted.

Were you an easy delivery for your mom?

I don't know, I'm adopted.

Did your mom get stretch marks? They're hereditary.

73

1. That's an odd question and 2. I don't know, I'm adopted.

People asked me "Are your parents...?" questions throughout my life in relation to anything from my height, my sensitive skin, my ever-expanding list of things I am allergic to, my skills and interests, and my career path. I suppose asking someone where they got a skill or interest can be categorized as casual conversation or an icebreaker.

You probably could file casual questions about heredity as, "Not too big of a deal," unless you are adopted, of course. The casual icebreaker, "Wow, you're tall, are your parents tall?" (aka "Who did you inherit your height from?") all of a sudden gets real deep when you respond, "I don't know, I'm adopted." Subsequently, curiosity wins over and a barrage of rather personal questions ensues. "Do you want to know your birth mother?" "Are you glad she gave you up?" "Do you think about her all the time?" "Why did she give you up?"

Post-reunion, I was able to answer questions for my second pregnancy like this:

How much did you weigh when you were born?

8lbs 6oz. Exactly one pound lighter than my firstborn.

Were you an easy delivery for your mom?

Nope.

Did your mom get stretch marks? They're hereditary.

1. That's an odd question and 2. I don't know. I'm not going to ask my mom about her stretch marks.

I don't feel guilty talking about heredity.

I have read in more than one research article that one common characteristic of closed adoption is that it can cause the adoptive parents to fear, or be intimidated by, the unknown biological family. As a result, the adoptee can begin to mirror this fear. My parents spoke very highly of this

74

mysterious woman who very much had a psychological presence in our home. Despite their actions, heredity was like the proverbial elephant in the room. It was hard for me to wonder aloud if something about me was learned from my adoptive parents, inherited it from my biological parents, or unique to me; a huge chunk of information was missing from the equation.

Post-reunion, now we know the answers to those questions. Believe it or not, knowing definitively what I inherited from my biological family has not made my adoptive family feel threatened. Rather, they learned what parts of me were inherent to me and received confirmation that they had done a good job nurturing what I was given Eliminating the secrets created by the nature of closed adoption and fostering an atmosphere of openness has improved my relationships with both of my families.

Something I still Cry About
How can you miss something you never had?

I love my conversations with one of my favorite adoptee friends. When she and I talk, we easily fall into the rhythm of "adoptee speak." One thing we talked about was how -- despite being reunited with our original families -- it was still very important to both of us to have any document or piece of our pre-adoption history. Having a solid piece of evidence that puts you at a certain place at a certain time is something that is important to many adoptees. My adoptee friend recently obtained more of her records from her adoption agency, which she found very validating. During the conversation, I was thinking of what I, too, wish I could have that were part of my experience pre-adoption, such as having the slightest clue of who my foster parents were or where in the world I was for the first four and a half months of my life. I would like to know that I did not drop off the face of the planet and that someone real loved me and took care of me. Then a lump rose in my throat when the next thought came into my head.

I want my bear. Where in the world is my bear?

I first found out that I was supposed to have a teddy bear when I unsealed my uncensored adoption file. I remember pouring through those records and stopping at the place where an adoption worker had recorded something to the nature of "the birth mother has purchased some things she would like to go with the baby. A small stuffed bear and a few outfits." I immediately telephoned my adoptive mother and the first words out of my mouth were, "Mom, do you know where my bear and outfits from my first mother are?" She told me that she was never given a bear or any outfits that were specified as being gifts from my original mother. I realize now she was caught off-guard by how devastated I seemed about a bear and clothing from nearly 25 years before.

I was devastated. Not having this simple, sweet gift from my mother, a piece of her to hold while I was growing up, was not just about the bear. It was about my sensitivity to her as one of my mothers and about how I, personally, identified with her as a mother myself. I remember how I chose every last thing that was purchased for my son before he was born with love and care. I wanted him to touch every blanket, hug every stuffed animal, look at every picture, and be surrounded by the warmth of everything around him knowing without a doubt that it all spelled out his parents' love for him. As a mother, I knew the thought, the love, and the anguish my first mother must have put into selecting this bear for me with her very best effort, trying to make sure it made its way to me. I imagined the faith she had put into this bear that it would comfort me on my journey; a companion for a journey she could not accompany me on. I knew in the very depths of my heart that this bear had meant something to her.

I worried when my first mother and I met face-to-face for the first time, that she would ask me about the bear. She did. At our reunion, my first mother opened her purse and pulled out a small plastic bag. Sealed inside for protection from the years was a picture of me as a newborn, the only photo of me that she had. The next thing she pulled out was my bear's "twin." She had carefully selected two bears, one that I would have and one that she would keep, so that we would always be connected, no matter where we were. She always kept her bear with her and she had assumed I was doing the same. It broke my heart to tell her that I never received my bear.

I cannot even fathom why my agency would not give me the bear from my first mother. A lot of adoption-related literature that I have read carries the conventional wisdom that at the time, it was not considered appropriate for the adoptive family to accept gifts and items from the original family. One source even said it was okay for adoption workers to tell the adoptee's original mother they would give an item to the adoptive parents to appease the mother. However, to actually do it was not acceptable because it was thought to be disturbing to the adoptive family.

Why is it that lying in adoption is not seen as wrong? Why did anyone not think it was unethical to tell my first mother they were going to pass along my gifts and then not do it? Perhaps my bear was just lost. Who could lose just a precious thing?

Of course, I wanted to share all of this with my friend at lunch, but this is the one thing about my adoption that I cannot talk about without crying. I am aware of how insignificant this must seem to outsiders looking in and perhaps how trivial it seems for me to be upset about, of all things, a teddy bear. I am thankful to have what I have and that my problems are not as catastrophic as those around the world. But I cannot help how I feel; I cannot stop the tears from coming to my eyes when I think about my bear, the little baby that went without it, and the very young mother who put every hope and prayer in that bear to love, protect, and comfort her child. I am reunited; I have my records and my original birth certificate.

But in an inexplicable way that perhaps is not understandable or even reasonable to most people...I want my bear.

Bearing Witness to Truth
Becoming a bridge between myth and reality in my adoption

"I couldn't find you because I didn't know your name," I said.

"Didn't know my name, but isn't it in your file or on your documentation?" she replied, shocked.

"Your name was taken off of my files. So was the name you gave me," I responded.

I almost could not say it. I almost could not finish the thought, "My birth certificate has my adoptive parents' names on it, not yours."

I had planned for how I was going to tell my original mother these details that made her unknown to me my entire upbringing. It was terrible, but straightforward enough. I could not find her because my records were amended and sealed. This is what many adoptees must overcome to find their original parents. This is what happens to all of our records.

I still choked with tears mid-sentence. It was wrong that she had never been told about this, especially before she consented to the adoption. I was effectively telling her that her motherhood had been erased and cast aside. I was put in the position of correcting the misinformation that she was given, that there was no openness to our adoption, and I could not just go and find her whenever I wanted.

Later that same day, I called my adoptive mother, who was eagerly awaiting an update on how my first contact with my original mother had gone. I braced myself to tell the other mother in my life something she, too, would be hurt to hear.

"The story that she wanted to 'move on with her life' wasn't really true, Mom." I started. "She thought our adoption was open. She signed those papers because she thought I could know who she was and reach out to her."

It was silent for a few moments.

"We didn't know that," she said. "We were told that we could have no contact with your family and that they didn't want us to anyway." She finished with a tone of anger in her voice, "If we had just known this could have caused her so much pain, we could have tried something. I don't know what. We had no idea who your family was, Amanda."

My adoptive mother expressed an overwhelming sense of compassion and devastation for how she knew the mother who shared her daughter must have been hurt by my silence and absence from her life. They never knew that she would have wanted to know me; that's not the story they were told. They were powerless to assuage the pain she felt not knowing where I was or if I was okay because they themselves were not given the whole story in order to make informed choices.

"What if she doesn't want to know you?" I think this is a question most adoptees are asked when they announce they are seeking reunion. The question I ask in return is, "What if she does?" Often times the closed adoption, the sealed records, and the secretive nature of adoption is seen as necessary to keep parties apart and from knowing each other "for their own good." This is the effect of adoption's secrecy legacy. When the adoptee conquers the odds and connects the severed ties between their families, they may take on the role of truth-teller. They become the one who must build bridges so that others can cross the caverns dug by adoption secrecy. As adoptees, what can we do when we discover truth and the grief of others so late in life? We join with our loved ones as they sit with their grief. We bear witness to their truth.

A Letter to my Unknown Foster Mother
Mother's Day is for you, too

Dear Unknown Foster Mother,

I have often wondered if you would remember me if we were to meet someday. I wonder if I was just one child, or one baby, that you cared for or if there were many more. How would I describe myself to you so that you would know which little baby was me? Then I remember a story my adoptive parents told me. They were told I did not have a name and they could not even meet you. On the day they came to your home to take me home with them, a little boy, maybe your son, slipped into the room to say goodbye. "Good bye, Sarah," he said. I imagine peeking over my father's shoulder at him as we disappeared through the doorway of your home, returning that goodbye in my own way.

My parents were perplexed as to where this name came from – was it a nickname? I know now that you named me Sarah. My legal name that my first mother lovingly gave to me was not used by my agency, except where legal matters were concerned. It is unlikely you were told what it was. So, you called me Sarah. It means "princess."

I did not realize the importance that you had in my life until I gave birth to my first son. In the first 5 months of his life, I took hundreds of photos of him. I wrote down his every move, chirp, and giggle. I nearly exploded with joy at every milestone because, like every mother, my baby was the strongest, smartest, and most beautiful child ever.

I was with you for my first five months of life. I have no pictures or mementos from that time. I often wonder if there are any. Your perceptions as the historian of my life during that time are unique. Your perspective was not one of observation to be added to a file somewhere. Your perspective was the kind that gets down on the floor with the child and makes silly faces until the child erupts with infectious laughter in the way only little babies can. That is something special.

81

When my first son was born, I found myself wanting to know more about my own birth. How much had I weighed? What did I look like? How long was I? My agency narrative was so bare and edited looking, and I had not yet realized I could unseal my adoption files. When I combed through my adoption file just one more time, a thin yellowed piece of paper was stuck between some photocopied sheets. Faintly jotted on this very small piece of paper were my birth statistics. My adoptive mother said, "Your foster mother must have slipped that in there before the file was given to us. I don't think she was supposed to do that, but she must have known you would want it."

Taking a stand, even in a small way, when it is the right thing to do is a part of themselves that all three of my mothers have given me.

Yes, you were, are, and forever will be a mother to me in some way. You are part of my narrative and personal journey through life. I celebrate you and my other mothers on Mother's Day. This day is for you, too.

Happy Mother's Day,
Amanda

Strange Compliments
What being told someone looks like me means to me

I begrudgingly pulled myself out of my chair and began the annoying task of packing up my books, notes, and other personal effects into my book bag. My dear book bag has been with me since the eleventh grade – ten years total – and barely shows any wear. I was about to cram my electronic tablet into my beloved red-with-black-trim pack when I heard my professor ask me if I had pictures of my kids "on that thing." Of course I did! Entering Proud Mama Mode, I switched on the device and showed him, and the other interested students still left in the room, a few pictures of my babies. Everyone agreed that my kids were super cute. My friend Deb began ushering me out the door when my professor observed:

"They look just like you."

"Thank you," I replied automatically.

"Was that a compliment?" he chuckled.

I paused.

"Well, it is to me," I responded.

"Oh?"

Another three second pause goes by. My friend Deb seemed torn between her quest to hurry me out the door and her desire to hear what I was going to say next.

"Yes. You know, I wasn't raised by my biological family." I explained. "No one ever said I looked like anyone else until recently. It makes me happy to hear people say that."

He smiled and shrugged as Deb, who was giving me her best lets-go-I'm-starving look, steered me by the elbow out of the classroom.

After this event, I began to think about what it meant to be told that I look like someone or that someone looks like me. It is a lot like being lost and encountering a kind soul along the way who recognizes me. It ties me to a history and a lineage that explains my existence. When my son, the first genetic relative I had ever seen, was born, I expected for any void I felt not having a biological connection to disappear. Seeing him, holding him, was a pivotal moment. Only instead of ushering in completeness, his birth awoke me to unanswered questions. I searched his face looking for mine only to find myself asking others, "Are you sure he looks like me?" Having not grown up

83

with people who shared my genetic makeup, I could not immediately tell which features he shared with me. Sometimes I still cannot.

My oldest son looks very much like his paternal aunt and my maternal aunt. My youngest son is the spitting image of his father. People innocently comment: "Wow, what ancestor did your son's hair color and eyes come from? He doesn't look like you at all!" and "Oh, I see daddy in that little one, but no mommy." Sometimes it stings. I hated hearing people make those observations about me as a child. I had cousins who looked like they could be my adoptive mother's daughters. They resembled her in ways of which I could only dream. "You don't look like your mom," though it means something different to my children, is honestly something I never wanted to hear said to my kids. So yes, my admirable professor, it is a compliment. You will never, ever know how much it means to me to hear that. I will never get tired of hearing it.

There are times in our lives when completely benign question causes us to think a million thoughts all at once. That was one of those moments.

The Mother-Daughter-Mother Connection
An end to adoption's nature vs. nurture debate

In the never-ending nature vs. nurture debate, adoptees are asked to pick whether nature or nurture provided more to them. This question often awkwardly implies that the adoptee must award the original family or the adoptive family with the coveted title of "best." I have had people question the validity of my adoptive connections because they are not supported by biology. I have had people question the validity of my biological connections because they are not supported by childhood nurture. What matters most is what a given adoptee decides her connections look like for herself, and no one but the adoptee can do this when it comes to their own story.

The idea that nature and nurture are diametrically opposed forces is present in adoption terminology discourse as well. Some mothers prefer to be called "natural mothers." This self-identified label is often mistaken for implying the opposite of the adoptive mother. It is said that if we call the original mother the "natural mother" then we are suggesting that the adoptive mother is "unnatural."

We must remember that every person has the right to self-identify and that group identification is about empowerment, not about implying negative things about others. The term "natural" far predates the "birth" label in terms of adoption policy and practice. Because some find the newer "birth" label offensive and the "biological" label to be distant and technical, "natural" is the term some mothers find feels right. The idea that this implies something negative including the "opposite" that the adoptive mother is "unnatural," signifies that the adoption community still views these mothers of adoption as enemies.

I do not view my mothers as enemies or opposites. Neither is more "real" than the other. Both women must be "real" in order for me to be "real." For me, one connection to one mother does not erase, overlap, or overpower the connection to the other. Each connection is made up of different components like memories, social history, biology, shared traits, shared interests, and shared experiences.

85

Each connection may be different, but they are a connection nonetheless. I cannot categorize or label either relationship. Love is fluid and infinite. I do not have less to give to one mother simply because I have given love to another.

I relate to each mother differently, but not in a way that needs to be seen as a competition between the two. We each have different needs, different strengths, and different challenges. Each mother is a different person that exchanges energy in our relationship in a different way.

The nature and nurture forces in my life are not opposed to each other; they are both irreplaceable parts of who I am. Nature is not the opposite of nurture. I have a natural mother and a nurturing mother. My genes – my nature – are not bad. My genes are not a foe to be conquered, but rather resources to be nurtured. Adoption discourse has become so focused on which force conquers the other that adoption practitioners have long failed to realize that these two elements of one's life are not opposed and enemies. They are a team. Reunion brings about the opportunity for those in closed adoptions to embrace this teamwork if all parties involved are willing to work to make it happen.

Part Three: Social Justice

"The good we secure for ourselves is precarious and uncertain until it is secured for all of us and incorporated into our common life." – Jane Addams

Adoption and Abortion
How intersection is different than being one in the same

Some activists in the reproductive justice realm, on both sides of limiting or expanding access to abortion, tend to shy away from reforming adoption policies and critically discussing adoption. Some may have very strong opinions that they believe adoption is an option for unplanned pregnancy, but lack an understanding of adoption's impact on those who live it. If their primary definition of adoption is that it serves as an alternative to abortion, they may be hesitant to question or change adoption policies, or may support bad policies based on how they feel it may impact abortion issues. This causes me to ask an obvious question – should people active within the abortion debate not expand their knowledge of adoption itself, within the framework of serving the needs of children, before forming their opinions?

Yes, there are women who become pregnant and do not wish to have abortions or parent. However, when this becomes every woman's story, we have created a stereotype. With stereotypes, we overlook the needs of women who have abortions for reasons relating to health and pregnancy, or who have unplanned pregnancies but wish to keep the babies born to them. When we make policies based on stereotypes, we run the risk of being oblivious to the net effect of a policy on the real people that our perception of an issue did not take into account.

The fact of the matter is, just because a given policy covers adoption does not mean it will address abortion issues. While there may be areas of intersection, completely conflating abortion with adoption may result in the formation of adoption policies that are also not what people impacted by adoption need. Therefore, blindly supporting something that carries the "adoption" label because you are passionate about the abortion debate is ill-advised.

Just a few United States based examples of questionable efforts aimed at increasing infant adoptions include: (1) bills that seek to limit the time period when adoption consents can be revoked, (2) campaigns that cherry-pick through research with questionable methods in order to portray one view of adoption, and (3) long-standing policies in some states that allow mothers to be asked to sign adoption consents before, or shortly after, giving birth.

These three efforts likely do contribute to an increase in adoption. The notion that expectant parents will sign irrevocable consents before they have held their child for the first time, or shortly thereafter, does not allow adequate time for those parents to make a decision. Additionally, campaigns that use isolated findings from less-than-credible research to make claims, such as, "100% of birth mothers choose the level of openness in their adoptions" (which defies the actual statute in every state) inspires a false reality of adoption.

When it comes to issues of informed consent, adequate time to make lifelong decisions, and respecting the right of children to be raised by their biological parents if and whenever possible, we have to have a deeper understanding of adoption itself to make good policy choices. When adoption's only story is a "solution" to another social issue, questionable campaigns and policies may not get the scrutiny they deserve.

If we do not properly scrutinize, we run the risk of not only missing our goal, but also of causing tandem problems. For example, the by-product of the abortion-adoption conflation equation has caused many pro-life advocates to oppose the right of adult adoptees to have access to their original birth record. Their thinking is that mothers of adoption are highly likely to hide their connection to adoption. As such, they would sooner have an abortion if they cannot be guaranteed that the birth record will be sealed. Adoptees are told they cannot be treated equally as a necessity to solve another social issue.

Yet, when states defy this stereotype and change policies to treat adoptees equally, abortion rates go down. In fact, abortion rates went down by 25% in Oregon after the state passed its historic adoption law that restored to adult adoptees access to their original birth certificates. This is just one area where it has been proven that the abortion-adoption stereotype is simply not a foundation for good policy.

The moral of this story is that abortion and adoption are not two versions of the same decision. Having an understanding of abortion issues does not mean you automatically have an understanding of adoption issues. Having an understanding of adoption issues does not mean you automatically have an understanding of abortion issues. Every issue involving the lives and welfare of human beings deserves attention and to not be understood by stereotypes. We must always seek to understand how issues intersect and how that intersection may intensify or complicate issues human beings may face. It

89

is important to realize that having a stance on abortion does not give you everything you need to know about adoption. There is still much to learn. Education is the vital key to change in every institution.

Am I Adopted at Work?
Something every adoption professional, adopted or not, needs to read

As an adoption activist, I am an "adoption worker" in the sense that I engage in advocacy for vulnerable people connected to adoption. However, I am not an adoption worker in the traditional sense. I do not counsel expectant parents or prospective adoptive parents. I do not have anything to do with the adoption facilitation process or even work within the child welfare system. It is ironic because people always say to me, "I bet you got into social work because you want to work in adoption and help other people have adoptions as wonderful as yours."

Adoption is not why I got into social work. Despite not being an adoption worker, the assumption that those connected to adoption desire to guide others into their own life's path needs to be addressed. Even without working in adoption, adoption does occasionally fall into my lap. When you work in social services, people will come to you with their problems even if it has nothing to do with your field or specialty. Sometimes, considering adoption is the topic that is presented.

Alternately, someone may have an issue that already involves adoption. For example, someone might have an adopted sibling with whom they would like to strengthen their relationship. They may come to a social worker they know or a social services agency with which they already interact.

The big question is: Do I even tell my clients that I am adopted? There are two big "nevers" of personal self-disclosure.

Never tell your client something for your benefit, especially if it is of no benefit to him.

Never tell your client anything that would compel them to feel sorry for you.

If I feel the need to tell someone I am adopted, I have to stop and ask myself, "Why do I want to tell them, and would it benefit them?" I need to be aware if my desire to disclose is because I need to get something off of my chest (not appropriate) or because I think it will help them in some way (appropriate).

There is a potential that by disclosing my adoption, I could cause some clients to feel sorry for me. Some people readily understand the issues of loss, gain, resiliency, and even ambiguity in adoption. Some people might not want to tell me how they really feel about the issue of adoption because they are afraid of hurting my feelings. Some people might project onto me how they believe the adoptee or potential adoptee in their life may turn out.

Self-disclosure in a professional setting is never automatic. It is done on a case-by-case basis, only when it is absolutely appropriate, and only when it is of specific benefit to the person seeking help.

It is hard to keep clients from knowing anything about me in rural social work and working in small towns. I see my clients outside of work on a regular basis and I am sure many of them know by now that I have an adoption connection. Some people may be really strengthened knowing that I am adopted. It may give them a sense of universality and comfort of having a shared experience with someone else. It simply depends on the situation.

Even if I did desire to go into adoption work, my adoption and feelings on it have no place in guiding the lifelong decisions of others. It does not matter what I think someone seeking help should or should not do. It is not my place to use my narrative to convince others to make the choices that I think they should make.

Social work is not about leading people in the way they should go. It is about recognizing the strengths within each person, and helping them interact with support systems to solve their problems. I do not go into my office every day thinking that I know better than my clients about their own lives. Social work is a partnership; it is an opportunity to walk side-by-side with someone who is struggling and give them someone to lean on while they choose the path that is best for them – no matter what the situation in life.

I realize in discussing this topic, I have bordered the line between conflating adoption work with social work. The distinction must be made that not all adoption workers are social workers. Perhaps if more adoption workers had social work values and upheld them, it would be an easier institution to fix and regulate. Bias is everywhere in private adoption literature with money and clients' competing interests involved. Social workers are trained to investigate their personal biases. I have never approached a helping agency of any sort thinking I had the answers everyone else should follow.

Ultimately, when it comes to talking about adoption with someone in my particular professional setting, it is never about me. It is not about my beliefs. It is not about my experience or perception. It is not about my feelings and it should never be made to be about me. This is the way I prefer to keep it.

A Letter to My Post-Adoption Social Worker
A letter I really wrote and really sent

Dear Post-Adoption Social Worker,

I am one of your agency's adoptees; you may be familiar with my name. A few years ago, you and I interacted because I was cautiously considering the idea of reunion. I wanted to reunite, but was afraid of hurting my adoptive family's feelings. I was also afraid that your agency would judge as being an "angry adoptee." I tried my best to communicate my feelings despite my fears. You were very kind in response, and I thank you for that. As I grow in my social work career, I cannot help but compare my social work knowledge, skills, and values to my own experience as a client of adoption. Adopted children are the most vulnerable individuals within an adoption system and therefore are an adoption worker's primary client. Helping professionals have the duty to secure the best interests of the child in adoption. According to multiple international conventions on human rights, a child's human rights include preservation of biological family whenever possible, heritage, and identifying family information. The NASW-PA itself has given written support for unrestricted adult adoptee access to original birth certificates.

Indeed, I am no longer a child. Yet despite being in the "child" role of the adoption system, I have never been treated by my adoption agency as a client of any sort. I received no post-adoption support (nor did my biological family or adoptive family) or on-going resources to help me make sense of my personal diversity in a non-adopted society. When I finally came back into contact with my agency some twenty years after my adoption, I once again was not regarded as a client. I have been effectively excluded from the client-practitioner system in my own adoption my entire life.

When I say that my "client" role was not acknowledged, I refer specifically to the fact that ethical guidelines that are meant to protect clients – and the values behind them – were not extended to me. The NASW Code of Ethics clearly dictates that clients be given access to their records. They only exception is in extreme circumstances when information would cause significant harm to that client. A fee schedule for

94

records access commodifies this right for clients based on class privilege. Non-identifying records, more accurately described as "censored records," also do not honor a client's right to information. Yet, this is what your agency offers to its adult adoptee clients.

Adult adoptees returning to their adoption agencies for information value the same things social workers value. What we want is very basic and simple. We want self-determination and autonomy. We want a respectful and inclusive definition of family where our inclusively defined family is seen as a strength rather than a weakness. We want transparency and truth. We want to know that the policies we encounter are based on empirical evidence and best practices that are healthy for us and respectful of our human rights. In summary, we simply ask for you to honor our dignity and worth as people.

When you responded to me saying, "Names were not exchanged at the time of your adoption" (which was a generalization and not my mother's actual wishes), and "I'll look in your file to see if there's anything in there that you can have," and later when another social worker sent me an expensive fee schedule, I felt like I was an intruder into my own adoption system rather than what I actually am – a client, a consumer, a participant. I have never had any say within this system that has profoundly impacted my life. You can imagine how disempowering that feels.

I do not blame you for not being able to give me my records. I understand that all of the agency professionals who my adoptive parents and I encountered at the agency during my quest for records access were just following agency policy. This is how adoption is for adoptees of my era. We are not considered clients. We are not even considered owners of our own birth experience. The fact that I once gazed into the eyes of the mother who birthed me means nothing. My cognitive stage of development at infancy that prevented me from recording her in permanent memory is held against me in the name of "confidentiality." What social workers can do is consider the inconsistency between agency post-adoption records access policies and the Code of Ethics/Core Social Work Values. We can work towards another one of our values, Social Justice, in places where it does not exist.

In case you might like to know, I did reunite. I am in a wonderful ongoing relationship with my first mother, 11 first aunts and uncles, and 26 first cousins and their children. I also have two brothers who have waited for me to return to the family their entire lives. It was you or another social worker who informed me that my first mother had contacted your agency when I was 18-years-old, but that you did not know why. So I asked my original mother. She was updating her information because she wanted to be contacted and wanted me to have my records. She was also seeking reassurance that her information had already been released to my adoptive family because she had expected to be in contact with me long before my 18th birthday.

In fact, her deciding factor in adoption had been that she was promised that I would know her and be able to contact her. She was convinced that openness, which did not actually exist in 1985, would make adoption less painful for her. She spent nearly twenty five years waiting for me around every corner and expecting my voice at the end of every phone call. She never gave up hope. What an amazingly strong woman she is.

Sincerely,
Amanda

My Amended Birth Certificate is a Lie
And why the lies need to stop

"Why would they lie?" I thought to myself when I first saw my amended birth certificate. I was 11- or 12-years-old and it was out on the kitchen counter for some reason. I was alone in the room at the time, wondering if I was allowed to look at the document. It occurred to me that I did not know my original mother's name. I wondered if I was even allowed to know. Feeling very brave and rebellious, I took a peek only to be taken aback that it did not contain my first mother's name at all. On my "certificate of live birth" were the names of my adoptive parents.

I immediately felt like the wind had been knocked out of me. Of course, I loved my parents and they were raising me. When I looked at my birth certificate, I was expecting to see birth information. I felt a deep sense of unfairness that my original mother's name had been removed from my birth certificate without anyone asking me what I wanted. I had no concept of an original existing elsewhere. Subsequently, I felt that any hope of ever knowing her or her name was removed from the table.

I was also struck by the profound departure this birth certificate represented from lessons most of us are brought up learning – that we should always tell the truth. Yet, my birth state had not been required to tell the truth. In fact, the state had put it on an official document, my birth certificate, while leaving off any mention that it was not the document with which I was born. The lesson I stood to learn in that moment was that perhaps there was something about adoption that made lying okay.

Birth certificates are not the property of adoption agencies. They are government recorded and issued documents. Every person who is born in the United States receives one when the vital statistics office of a given state collects certain information at their birth. Birth certificates have come to be used as a method of proving identity. When a child is issued a decree of adoption, which could be months or years after her birth, she receives an amended certificate. The amended certificate presents the adoptive parents as though they are the original parents and makes no mention that it is not the original document. At the time of writing this book, adoptees in forty-four states do not have the same access to the birth certificates that they were born with that everyone else receives.

Some people claim that the amending and sealing of adoptee birth records makes it easier for the adoptive parents. They can present the amended certificate to prove their child's identity without having to explain to nosey people that the child was adopted. When adoptees become adults and want to know the names of their original parents, obtain a driver's license or passport, vote, or obtain job security clearance, however, they may have difficulty doing so. Whatever limited convenience amending and sealing offers is outweighed by the fact that these sealed birth certificates may become a lifelong inconvenience for many adoptees.

Some people claim that birth certificates must be sealed to prevent unsavory information about the original family from surfacing. We must first remember what purpose birth certificates serve in the first place. Birth certificates are a historical document meant to capture information from the moment in history when a person was born. They are not "hide your family drama" certificates. No person, regardless of family issues, has their original birth certificate sealed, unless they are adopted. When we specifically delineate adoption as being "more dramatic" than any other life circumstance, to the point where it needs to be hidden, we send a terrible message about being adopted.

Not only does my amended birth certificate contain information that is not true, it facilitates lying. In addition to claiming that my adoptive parents gave birth to me, my amended birth certificate also states that it is the true and original document on file with the state registrar. Its filing date is not the date on which it was filed, but the date on which the original birth certificate was filed. I did not officially meet my parents until almost five months after my birth, and was not adopted until January of the following year. Yet my amended birth certificate with their names on it states that my birth record was filed one month after I was born. In essence, there is nothing about this document that would compel adoptive parents to tell their children about their adoption.

Amended birth certificates become increasingly problematic in transracial and inter-country adoptions. These certificates claim that the – often times white – adoptive parents gave birth to the person of color. Amended certificates may reflect the residential town of the adoptive parents, rather than the place of birth. Often times, the race listed on the amended birth certificate may be altered to reflect the race of the adoptive parents. First Nations adoptees are denied membership and benefits of their tribes without documentation proving they were born to a tribe member.

My original mother did not know what amending and sealing was when I we first reunited. She expressed shock that my adoptive parents' names had taken the place of her name on my new birth certificate. I reflect on the mistruth of the amended certificate when I think of my own mother. By the state replacing her name on my birth certificate, she is forced into a lie when her motherhood is erased.

Although my adoptive parents did know about amending and sealing, they did not realize that I would not be able to access my original birth certificate when I turned 18-years-old. They, too, had been forced into a lie. Putting their names on my birth certificate "normalized" our family by making it appear that we had a biological connection. It sends the message that I cannot be viewed as their daughter unless we make it seem like they gave birth to me.

The practice of amending and sealing itself was founded on telling lies. The very first birth records that were sealed were of illegal adoptions that illegally practicing adoption workers like a woman named Georgia Tann were trying to hide. Not only were birth certificates initially sealed to keep original families and adoptive families from connecting to reconcile the illegal seizure of children from their homes and subsequent illegal adoptions, it became part of a marketing campaign. Counter to the "bad blood" stereotypes that kept people from adopting orphaned and abandoned children, Tann billed children as a fresh start and blank slate to be shaped by their adopting parents. Amended and sealed birth records were a large part of the idea that the adoptees original, illegitimate identity was a thing of the past.

The amending and sealing of birth records exemplifies H. David Kirk's "shared fate" theory, specifically what he referred to as "rejection of difference." According to Kirk, adoptive families have been told to cope with their difference from biological families by rejecting that there is a difference. Adoptive families may also attempt to mirror biological families by adopting infants, add children to their family in a way that mirrors biological birth order, and be matched with their adopted children by appearance. If we accepted adoptive families the way that they are, we would not have to enforce this coping mechanism of denial in how we handle adoptee records and identity.

It is an established right of children to have a name from birth and to retain access to their heritage. It is the established right of adopted children to have their original information preserved on their behalf, yet few state laws recognize the right for the adoptee to access it. We certainly cannot force every adoptive parent to be open about the adoptee's origins as the adoptee is growing up. However, we can ensure that the government is not participating in the deception of adoptees by altering and sealing their records.

Adoptees should have the same access to their birth records that those who are not adopted receive. We should not hand adoptees documentation that has been altered, making factual copies inaccessible to them, and expect them not to feel slighted. The measure of how well someone is "adjusted" to being adopted should not be their ability to accept that their biology has been scourged from the record. Adoptive families, original families, State legislators, and our allies need to stand hand-in-hand with adoptees and send the message loud and clear – no more lies.

The Beauty of a Single Story
The sacred duty of honoring someone's story

I have been working in health care and social services related fields off and on for several years. During this time, I have had countless opportunities to write case notes, and read case notes written by others. Shorthand over the years has caused health care practitioners to frame "what someone struggles with" as being "the label of who they are." Time constraints, enormous caseloads, and character limits in data entry systems turn, "Mr. Smith becomes more agitated in the evenings and benefits from reassurance and comforting" to "Mr. Smith is a 'sundowner.'" It is true that in a professional setting, shorthand is sometimes impossible to get around. I have been trying to make a sincere effort to note in a way that explains the strengths a client uses to get around their struggles, rather than using a struggle as a label. Why is this so important to me?

I respect that every client has a right to read their record.

When a client reads their record, I want it to truly reflect how I see them. I do not see my clients as a list of problems that need to be fixed, but as a person with honest struggles and also strengths that can be used to overcome those struggles. This is why it is important to write the truth. Clients of social workers have the right to see their records, but also to know what has been recorded about them is true.

The title of this essay is in honor of a beautiful speech by Chiamanda Adiche entitled, "The Danger of a Single Story." Adiche warns against only telling a single story of a person or group because it becomes the entire picture of who they are to the rest of the world. When I write case notes, sometimes I am only ever able to tell a single story about a client. Yet, in the spirit of Adiche's words, I do not take this duty, the portrayal of the person whom I am writing about, lightly. For clients who have been alienated by friends and family, or who are older and have lost the majority of their loved ones over the year, I realize that I may be the only one in a given point in time who is recording their story.

As a client of adoption, I did not get to see my adoption record until I was almost 25 years old. I asked my agency if I could see it several times years prior and was told no. These were my files, describing my pre-adoption life and experience, with my name on them. They are mine. When I finally obtained my files, it was after a long and expensive legal process through my birth state's confidential intermediary. I had to have special permission for my own file to not be heavily censored. I do not know very many adoptees who can go back to their agencies or other adoption facilitators and get their records.

I wanted my records for a variety of reasons. Mostly, I wanted to see what someone had written about me during the "unknown" gap in my life. The time period from three-days-old when I was surrendered to foster care for adoption to nearly five-months-old when I went home with my adoptive parents was missing from my memories. Just as the notes I have taken on my clients may be the only pieces of their history in that moment in time that will ever be recorded, the workers overseeing my care had the privilege of holding the narrative of a little baby girl in their hands.

What my adoption workers recorded about me would be the only things written or known about my history during that time. What I received nearly 25 years later, noted on that five months of my history, was a few sentences about soy formula, sunburn, and one partial medical record. I will likely never know the names of my foster parents or my very first pediatricians who could be oral historians of my early life. The story of the bubbling baby girl is gone forever.

Those of us who have finally obtained our files know that information was not always found to be written person-first-positively. When you put the person first in how you write about them, you voice their strengths and challenges in a way that honors their dignity and worth as a human being. In some adoption records, our mothers, our adoptive parents, and we were written as simply cases that needed to be "solved." Some information between the verbal narrative from agencies and facilitators and what is found to be documented in files later on are not congruent. When we approach legislators who are not signed-on to the idea of transparency in adoption, we have to ask, "What exactly was being noted about us that we can't see?"

I had the privilege of supporting a dear friend who fought a long, hard battle to access the files that, by all helping professional standards, had always belonged to him. His battle for his records could have started sooner if he had only been told he was adopted, rather than discovering it in his 40s during an ordeal applying for his passport. Upon receiving his records, he immediately did a search for his original mother. By the time this dear man found his mother, she had been deceased for nearly two decades. This man lost his mother three times; once at birth, once when he discovered his adoption, and once when he found her grave.

My heart aches when I reflect on his story. His self-determination, a fundamental value social workers uphold for their clients, was completely negated. Withholding his rights from him only intensified his adoption losses and the loss of the mother who, per the family, wanted to know him, but died before she could meet him. What is the reason for this? What purpose did sealing these records and ultimately facilitating the lies that were told to this man serve? Clients of helping professionals have a right to see what is being noted about them. If our stories were written well, with all of the respect and care our humanity entitles us to, there is no reason not to give us access to our records. What is it specifically that is so terrible for us to see? When adopted people are specifically exempt from this treatment, we fail to extend to them the ethical protections guaranteed to clients and the benefit of the values behind them.

The Tragic Narrative
Coming to self-affirming conclusions in spite of tragedy

Dear Amanda,

I just found out that I was conceived from rape. What do I do now?

Signed, A Blog Reader

After disclosing that I was conceived from rape on my blog, I have received dozens of emails similar to this one. Adoptees, their original and adoptive parents, and their spouses frequently ask me where help and support can be found for adoptees who are coming to terms with a conception circumstance like rape or incest. They also want to know how I reached a place where I can talk about it openly.

I cannot answer their question as well as I would like because, outside of my adoptive parents and my original family, I never received any support regarding my conception circumstances. When I research the topic to try to answer the question of where support can be found, I find an abundance of political websites. There are few accessible organizations and entities providing support to adoptees outside of providing a platform for adoptees conceived from rape to use their narratives in support of the pro-life movement.

I never wanted to publically disclose my conception circumstances, but the politicizing of the issue made it necessary. The focus of available support for someone conceived from rape is almost exclusive to what they can give to politics, rather than what they can actually receive in universality, acceptance, and support. I find this to be deeply troublesome, and I speak out because people deserve better than this. When someone discovers this tragedy in their narrative they deserve to find one source that is compassionate and not mocking. These individuals and their families need to know that their value as people far exceeds what politics co-opts from their stories.

There are some truths that have been vital to me in my healing. I hold to them daily and my small contribution to those with sexual violence in their narrative is to put them into writing and pass them along.

I define who I am.

What an ancestor did is not who I am. I am not a bad seed and I do not have flawed genes. I am a mother, friend, and ally to many. I am not the phrase "should have/could have/would have been aborted." You should assume that I am a source of strength within the relationship with my original mother well before you assume that I am a "painful reminder" that she had to work to accept. I am stronger than the challenges in my life and I will take that fact and work to end child abuse, sexual violence, and unethical adoption practices. I am many things in one person and greater than the sum of my parts. Everyone is.

I am equally human.

As a human being, I am entitled to equal treatment under the law, respect for my feelings, and the same identity rights afforded everyone else. When it comes to allowing adult adoptees access to identifying information about their origins, including their own government recorded birth certificates, people conceived from rape or incest can get left behind. Leaving us out has been a concession some activists have been willing to make. My own birth state discriminates against my birth certificate access because of my conception circumstances. This is not acceptable.

Other people's ignorance is not my problem.

There are bio-essentialist people in the world who believe that everyone's actions are biologically determined and that we are all condemned by the actions of our parents. There are people who will never offer us support, but will still feel perfectly entitled to our sensitive narratives when it comes to their own political gain. The news media will likely continue to report irreverently on us and our mothers. This is their ignorance and I feel sorry for them. We cannot allow it to impact how we feel about ourselves.

Give myself permission to let go of the anger.

My original mother has told me that she forgave him as a way of being able to fully love me. What he did was wrong, yet I have let go of the anger because I cannot let his horrible actions make me bitter. Bitterness is a fire that consumes the person who harbors it.

Embrace my family and ancestry.

Just as I am not condemned by what my biological father did, I cannot condemn my ancestors or denounce my ancestry. Through my original paternal family, I have a rich German and Irish heritage as well as grandparents of whom I am proud. I also have a wonderful relationship with my paternal aunt that I would not trade for the world.

Work to understand sexual violence.

Part of acknowledging that I am not doomed by "bad genes" or condemned to feel ashamed of myself for what my biological father did, is coming to understand the causes of sexual violence in our society. I had the privilege to discuss the concept of "evil" with an adoptee who was also conceived through rape and whose adoptive father was murdered later on in her life. She wrote to me in an email (published here with permission),

One thing that I have learned is that if I call someone evil-like the man that got my mother pregnant or the man that killed my adopted father-I almost make it so they aren't responsible because I have made them inhuman. The fact is they are human and they did really bad/evil things.

My biological father was not a monster or a bad, evil person who was born broken. He was a real person who had real problems and who did something that has no justification. He had stressors in his life and subsequently acted out in an inappropriate and inexcusable way. Nevertheless, as the adoptee I quoted pointed out, pretending that men who commit rape are born broken and inhuman erases their culpability for their actions. It removes the responsibility of all people to create a healthy society that works to prevent rape from happening.

Ultimately, persons conceived from rape must embrace their self-worth and their entitlement to rights. We can work for others to understand our needs and the ignorance we may face in society and the media. We can be helped by understanding the systemic stressors surrounding human beings that cause them to do evil things. We can embrace the family that we do have and allow them to be sources of strength in our lives. Those who love us and are entrusted with the task of telling us about our conception must affirm our self-worth to us every day. None of us are condemned "just because" or by genes. I speak daily to these truths.

About the Author

Amanda H.L. Transue-Woolston is a reunited adult adoptee. She was born in 1985 and surrendered to private adoption at three days of age. Her adoption agency placed her in foster care before she was placed with her adoptive parents at nearly five months of age and officially adopted at 8 months old. Her adoption was finalized in 1986 and facilitated by the largest adoption agency in the United States.

Amanda was born and adopted in the United States. She is white, and was adopted by a married heterosexual couple of the same race. She was raised in a Christian, politically conservative, middle-class home in a small town. Her adoption was closed and her agency narrative was a short, heavily edited description of her origins.

She started her blog in hope that her original family could come across it and contact her. She also attempted to locate her original family through her agency with no success. Finally, she engaged with her birth state's confidential intermediary system. Bewildered and emotionally drained by the systemic issues and ugly stereotypes that stood as barriers to her information, she began blogging about how the backwards adoption policies she encountered affected her. Her writing has long focused predominantly on the surreptitious manner in which adoption records and birth certificates are handled and the negative messages this standard of secrecy sends about being adopted.

She became "declassified" when her government-held adoption file and original birth certificate were released to her in 2009. She reunited with her original mother, brothers, and extended maternal original family and one paternal aunt in January of 2010. Her biological great-grandmother and adoptive grandmother are also adult adoptees. In May 2013, Amanda changed her legal name to include surnames of her families by birth, adoption, and marriage. Concurrent with these enormous life events, Amanda returned to school to obtain a Bachelor's degree in social work. Her academic experience was integral in unfolding as a policy activist, writer, and professional.

Amanda is a social worker, author, speaker, award-winning blogger, feminist, and adoption activist. She has given insight, testimony, and criticism on adoption policies in more than eight states and is a board member of three adoption policy grassroots initiatives. Her writing on adoption has been published in six books, including her own book, and the Lost Daughters (November 2013) anthology of which she is the primary editor.

She was a featured mom activist on Mother's Day on Yahoo! Voices and was named in the "Top 20 Adoption Blogs" list and on the "Blogs We Love" list at Adoptive Families Magazine.

Amanda has an AA in Psychology from Harford Community College and a BSW from West Chester University. She is currently an advanced standing candidate for an MSS in Clinical Social Work at Bryn Mawr College. She lives with her husband and two children in the Greater Philadelphia Area.

39390127R00067

Made in the USA
Lexington, KY
20 February 2015